ation, Market Archetypes
and Outcome

Soumodip Sarkar

Innovation, Market Archetypes and Outcome

An Integrated Framework

With 70 Figures and 15 Tables

Physica-Verlag

A Springer Company

Soumodip Sarkar
University of Évora
Department of Management
Largo de Colegiais No. 2
7000-803 Évora
Portugal
ssarkar@uevora.pt

Library of Congress Control Number: 2007925176

ISBN 978-3-7908-1945-8 Physica-Verlag Heidelberg New York

Physica-Verlag is a part of Springer Science+Business Media

springer.com

© Physica-Verlag Heidelberg 2007

Production: LE-TEX Jelonek, Schmidt & Vöckler GbR, Leipzig
Cover-design: WMX Design GmbH, Heidelberg

SPIN 12021932   134/3100YL - 5 4 3 2 1 0   Printed on acid-free paper

Preface

If there is an award for one word that captures the imagination of academia, the media, businesses, as well as politicians, one strong contender must be the word "innovation". This word holds the promise of unlocking the gates to enhancing firm productivity and promoting economic growth. "Innovation" is also the Holy Grail of the corporate world.

It is difficult to open a business journal or attend a seminar without somebody throwing "innovation" at us. A quick (non scientific) search reveals the astronomical number of times that "innovation" appears in the online media, as of January 25th 2006 – 131 million references! This phenomenon can be seen from the figure below which reveals this trend of the frequency of online visibility of "innovation".

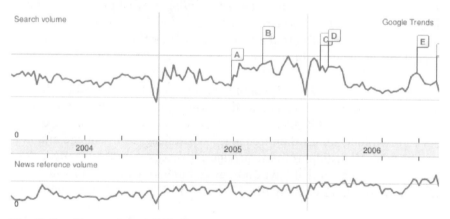

Fig. Online "innovation visibility"
Source: Google trends

Except for the "flat earth" equivalent of academics, there can be little doubt that innovation holds the key to unlocking firm competitiveness and growth. Yet, innovation is shrouded in a cloud of haze. Starting from its proper definition, and brushing aside management buzzwords swarming over the word, any serious study of innovation leaves one with more questions than answers…

This book is the spin off of my research into one question - can there be one framework that enables an understanding of innovation-market outcome linkages? Innovation literature is rich in typologies and descriptions of innovation dynamics, but is largely technology focused. The complex and profound interplay between strategy, innovation, markets and outcome is missing. And it was this that I had been seeking.

My research and my own varied background, led me to a way to explain this interplay – in the form of what I call the integrated innovation model.

This framework permit the academic, the management consultant and the manager alike to understand 'where' a product (or a single product firm) is located in an integrated innovation space, a space defined by market structure, degree of innovation and market outcome; 'why' it is so located and which then provides valuable clues as to 'what' to do while designing strategy. The model also explains much of the dynamics surrounding changing external climate and internal strategies. The integration of most of the important determinant variables in one visual framework with a robust and an internally consistent theoretical basis is an important step towards devising comprehensive firm strategy. The integrated framework provides vital clues towards framing a 'what to' guide for managers and consultants. Furthermore, the model permits metrics and consequently diagnostics of both the firm and the sector and this set of assessment tools provide a valuable guide for devising strategy.

I was never ambitious. At school I would envy my hard working friends who had all the answers and made their parents happy! I put it down to my lack of desire to be 'like them'- meaning people who want to please others. As I grew older, things didn't change. My colleagues in college and university were all fastidious folks, striving for success. I put down my lack of motivation as a sign that I was not an ambitious man! And this rationale has continued all through my life. Until recently. I have become ambitious.

An ambition to try to explain the strategy-innovation-outcome- market dynamics using a single analytical framework. The task was ever more ambitious because I didn't want to restrict myself to the theoretical part, but to apply the framework to trying to explain many of the issues I felt are important in a study of innovation and markets. I wanted to study cases and apply the cases. Once I started on this journey, every piece of business news, I would see and try to explain through the lens of the integrated model!

This book is not a book about the innovation process, nor does it have a new set of taxonomy or classification of innovation types. Nor do I research the sources of innovation. It is also not meant to serve as a how to guide. It is simply a book that explains innovation and market linkages, and along the way, uses a unified framework to explain a variety of market dynamics using actual cases whenever possible. I also believe this book to be a work in progress....there is so much more to understand and explain!

There are a few people to whom I am extremely grateful for. First of course is my research assistant, Paulo Ferreira, to whom I am grateful for the research assistance, his patience and dedication. I also thank him for putting up with my own fastidiousness. I am also grateful to Isaura Paulino for identifying typesetting errors. The scope of the book required immense research and I am sure that despite my best efforts, there remain some errors, factual or otherwise. I am solely responsible for them.

I also want to thank Dwight Perkins for his support and the Asia Center at Harvard University where I spent part of my sabbatical researching this book. I am grateful to Dan Lomba for his friendship and hospitality during my stay in Boston. My thanks also go to the science foundation of Portugal (FCT) for the financial assistance I received during the course of writing this book. And finally I want to thank my family- my wife Cesaltina Pires and our kids Vasco, Raul, Bruno and Joana for putting up with me!

I dedicate this book to all those seemingly forever in the twilight zone, wanting to understand.

February 2007   Soumodip Sarkar

Contents

1 Innovation

Just as energy is the basis of life itself,
and ideas the source of innovation,
so is innovation the vital spark of all human
change,
improvement and progress.

Attributed to *Theodore Levitt*

1.1 What Is Innovation?

If there is a popularity award for a word that captures the imagination of academia, politicians, media and businesses alike, one strong contender that stands out is the word "*innovation*". Coupled with "*entrepreneurship*", it holds the promise of unlocking the gates to the opening of new markets, enhanced firm efficiency and economic growth.

The word "innovate" is derived from Latin, *in+novare*, that is to "make new", to renew or to alter. Put simply, innovation is about having and applying a new idea, or sometimes applying other peoples ideas in new and novel ways (see Box 6.2). As aptly noted by Michael Vance:

> "Innovation is the creation of the new or the re-arranging of the old in a new way."

Many of the products that we consider to be innovative are often based on ideas of others or a rework of existing products in a way that turns out to be a hit with consumers (think iPod). In a mundane sense at many points in our lives, we are all innovators. The challenge arises when innovation is about an idea that is implemented successfully resulting in a positive outcome. For a firm this connected to the launching new products or improving on an existing product. Sometimes it involves organisational innovation that enhances firm efficiency. At a macro level, innovation is intimately connected to economic growth and welfare.

Although innovation may be intimately linked to technology, it doesn't necessarily have to have technology at the core. If the market accepts a new idea, and a firm is successful in transforming this new idea into a product that sells in the market place, then that is innovative. In the world of fashion, an outrageous costume (that nobody will ever wear) is considered innovative. Indeed the fashion world is driven by the constant drive to be innovative, which has often to do with the shock appeal. However technology by making a product difficult to being imitated provides the *stickiness* as well as potential for much higher growth that in turn provides sustainability to innovation (see Box 5.3).

Innovation has a broad canvas, including involving social change that need not involve technology. For instance the micro-credit model (pioneered by Muhammad Yunus who was honoured with the 2006 Nobel Peace Prize) which is an instrument in the fight against poverty, is also innovation. Innovation that involves reworking the business model need not directly involve technology.

So what again is innovation? Succinctly, innovation is the exploitation of new ideas which find market acceptance, often incorporating new technologies, processes, design and best practices. The innovation process generally involves the following phases:

- having a new idea or rethinking an old one
- recognising opportunities that exist or can be promoted
- choosing the best alternatives
- application of the idea and the process.

In *Winning at New Products*, Cooper[1] describes a structured process for new product development. The stages involve:

- Scoping: A quick desk research phase
- Building the business case
- Design and development
- Testing and validation
- Launch stage, where the product is commercialized.

---

[1] See Cooper (2001).

Importantly Cooper calls for the installation of *gates* where bad ideas get weeded out. These gates serve as checkpoints at the end of each stage, as shown in Fig 1.1.

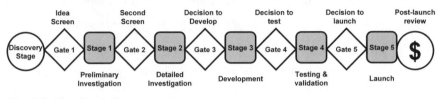

Fig. 1.1. The *Stage Gate* process

For a historical definition of innovation, one must turn to Joseph Schumpeter (1883-1953) who held technological change to be one of the major determinants of industrial transformation, and consisted of the introduction of new products (product innovation), new production processes (process innovation) and new management methods (organisational innovation). Schumpeter's definition of innovation was based upon the notion of the production function. As he noted[2]:

> "We will now define innovation more rigorously by means of the production function previously introduced. As we know, this function describes the way in which quantity of product varies if quantities of factors vary. If, instead of quantities of factors, we vary the form of the function, we have an innovation. But this not only limits us, at first blush at least, to the case in which the innovation consists in producing the same kind of product that had been produced before by the same kind of means of production that had been used before, but also raises more delicate questions. Therefore, we will simply define innovation as the setting up of a new production function. This covers the case of a new commodity, as well as those of a new form of organization such as a merger, for the opening up of new markets, and so on. Recalling that production in the economic sense is nothing but combining productive services, we may express the same thing by saying that innovation combines factors in a new way, or that it consists in carrying out New Combinations, although, taken literally, the latter phrase would also include what we do not now mean to include, namely, those current adaptations of the coefficients of production which are part and parcel of the most ordinary run of economic routine within given production functions."

Schumpeter distinguished between the trilogies of *invention, innovation* and *diffusion* (see Box 1.1). Interestingly Schumpeter's perspective of who

---

[2] See Schumpeter (1939).

is an entrepreneur is exactly the same as that of an innovator. He argued that the entrepreneur is the innovator who implements change within markets through the carrying out of new combinations. The new combinations could manifest itself as the one or a combination of the following:

- The introduction of a new good or quality thereof
- The introduction of a new method of production
- The opening of a new market
- The conquest of a new source of supply of new materials or parts
- The carrying out of the new organization of any industry

Management guru Peter Drucker explicitly calls for the entrepreneur to equip himself with the tool of innovation[3], when he declared that[4]:

> "Innovation is the specific tool of entrepreneurs, the means by which they exploit change as an opportunity for a different business or a different service. It is capable of being presented as a discipline, capable of being learned, capable of being practiced. Entrepreneurs need to search purposefully for the sources of innovation, the changes and their symptoms that indicate opportunities for successful innovation. And they need to know and to apply the principles of successful innovation."

In a similar vein, Freeman and Soete (1997) couples entrepreneurship with innovation, declaring the latter to be:

> "The first commercial application or production of a new process or product, it follows that the crucial contribution of the entrepreneur is to link the novel ideas and the market."

---

[3] However some authors believe that Drucker did not necessarily view the two as the same. J. Gregory Dees writing in *The Meaning of Social Entrepreneurship* noted that: "For Drucker, starting a business is neither necessary nor sufficient for entrepreneurship. He explicitly comments. Not every new small business is entrepreneurial or represents entrepreneurship. He cites the example of a husband and wife who open another delicatessen store or another Mexican restaurant in the American suburb as a case in point. There is nothing especially innovative or change-oriented in this."

[4] See Drucker (1993).

Box 1.1: When what we want is the weed

It is well know that many ideas, brilliant at first sight, often either never go beyond the drawing board, or quickly die in the market place. As we shall repeatedly encounter in this book, *outcome* and the *sustainability of innovation* are central themes that run all through the chapters of this book. Metcalfe (1999) said it best when he noted that "invention is a flower, innovation is a weed."

The Schumpeterian trilogy divided technological change into three stages. Schumpeter identified the first stage as involving the invention process, encompassing the generation of new ideas. The second stage was the innovation process encompassing the development of new ideas into marketable products and processes. The last was the diffusion stage, and this third stage was marked by the spread of new products and processes spread.

As reported by authors Bobrow and Shafer (1987), this failure rate can reach an astounding 48% for new products! In his entertaining book Franklin (2003) exploring why innovation fails, he gives instances how simple oversights or mistakes can result in failure. Thus the $125 million *Mars Climate Orbiter* satellite launched in December of 1998 failed because of the usage of the English measurement units and not metric!

If one was to seek some more formal definitions of innovation, there are plenty for company. For instance the Oslo Manual of the OECD (2005) makes a distinction between product and process innovation as follows:

> "(1) A product innovation is the introduction of a good or service that is new or significantly improved with respect to its characteristics or intended uses. This includes significant improvements in technical specifications, components and materials, incorporated software, user friendliness or other functional characteristics." (2) "A process innovation is the implementation of a new or significantly improved production or delivery method. This includes significant changes in techniques, equipment and/or software."(3) "A marketing innovation is the implementation of a new marketing method involving significant changes in product design or packaging, product placement, product promotion or pricing." (4) "An organisational innovation is the implementation of a new organisational method in the firm's business practices, workplace organisation or external relations."

Each researcher tends to define innovation often based on his perspective on what is the most important aspect of innovation. Hence according to the authors Tidd et al (1997), innovation is:

> "A process of turning opportunity into new ideas and of putting these into widely used practice."

Whereas for Cumming (1998), the emphasis is on originality, when he defined innovation as:

> "The first successful application of a product or process."

Rogers (1962): defined and characterized innovation from the user perspective, presenting five criteria for (user based) innovation:

> "Relative advantage: Do people think it is an improvement over what already exists?
> Compatibility: Is it consistent with the values, experiences and needs of the people who might adopt it?
> Complexity: Will potential users find it easy to use and understand?
> Trialability: Can people experiment with the innovation before deciding to adopt it?
> Observability: How easy is it for people to see its results?"

Meanwhile Wikipedia, the brilliant example of what is now termed to be *open source* innovation, defines innovation as follows:

> "The classic definitions of innovation include: 1) the process of making improvements by introducing something new; 2) the act of introducing something new: something newly introduced; 3) the introduction of something new; 4) a new idea, method or device; 5) the successful exploitation of new ideas; 6) change that creates a new dimension of performance."

Box 1.2: Innovation from developing countries

Today, innovation is no longer confined to the developed economies. Many innovative enterprises both in the industrial as well as in the service sector are fast emerging from developing economies like India, China, Russia, Brazil, Philippines etc. Developing countries have not normally been associated with the dynamic use and development of technologies, but are now becoming increasingly successful in both technological parity and endogenous technology creation. Take the case of a developing country like Brazil, no more than 9% of whose manufactured exports are high technology products has now established a successful civil aircraft manufacturing industry. The rapidly rising software export from India is another example. Outsourcing of services to countries like India is no longer about cost reduction, but about sourcing innovation. Innovation leaders like Microsoft are now establishing R&D centres in countries like China and India from where some of its most important products are emerging.

The emphasis on investment in innovation, especially in Asia, is beginning to bear fruit. The share of global high-tech exports from Asian developing economies rose from 7% in 1980 to 25% in 2001. At the same time, the U.S. share f global high tech exports declined from 31% to 18%, according to the U.S. National Science Foundation (2005). Another telling indicator is that of the Asian share of all published scientific papers climbed from 16% in 1990 to 25% in 2004. Clearly over the following years, we shall increasingly witness developing countries, especially from Asia, leading innovation.

1.2 Why Innovate?

> "Any business faces two basic demands: it must
> execute its current activities to survive today's
> challenges and adapt those activities to survive
> tomorrow's...The evidence suggests that most
> companies are far better at the executing half of
> the dialectic than at the adapting half."
>
> *The McKinsey Quarterly: The Adaptable
> Corporation*

In a knowledge-based economy firms must develop new products and services to increase turnover. In today's business environment, given acute competition and the overall market instability, for firms to remain competitive and profitable, they must keep developing new ideas and concepts to keep ahead of the competition. It is only through innovation that firms can create value and differentiate their products and services from that of the competition. In a global economy competitive advantage is achieved via the access to the best research and thought leaders. Liberalization of trade-both merchandise as well as in financial markets, coupled with technological advances in information and communications technologies (ICTs), have greatly reduced geographic and trade barriers, leaving firms and countries ever more vulnerable to international competition. This reinforces the necessity for firms to innovate continually, adapt and create new products, services and entire business models, to compete beyond regional borders.

Technological progress according to the Nobel economist Robert Solow, has a strong influences economic growth. Nations compete to attract innovative firms, for greater job growth and to improve productivity. A more innovative economy makes a greater investment in both people as well as in capital and has a greater capacity to attract and retain highly qualified people.

The correlation between innovative capacity and performance to economic development has been further strengthened over the recent decades. Recent studies indicate that technological progress is now responsible for up to one half of the growth of the US economy[5]. In most countries the success and growth of small and medium sized firms is connected with innovation.

At a firm level, studies point out to a positive correlation between innovation efforts as measured by R&D expenditure to outcome. A study by the British Department of Trade and Industry (DTI) – *The R&D Scoreboard 2006*, found that the links between R&D and business performance show up in wealth creation efficiency, sales growth and market capitalization[6].

The study noted the positive impact of R&D expenditure which showed up in the:

---

[5] Schacht (2000).
[6] See www.innovation.gov.uk/rd_scoreboard/executive.asp

"Above average wealth creation efficiency is associated with above average investment intensity (R&D and Capex). In both the 2005 and 2006 Value Added Scoreboards, for the 12 sectors where R&D and Capex investment is significant, over 75% of companies having above average wealth creation efficiency also had above average investment intensity. Higher R&D intensity has been positively linked to higher sales growth... It is of particular interest that many leading companies in their sectors invested more heavily during recessions than their less successful peers."

However using R&D alone is no guarantee of innovation success. Booz Allen & Hamilton's annual study of the world's 1,000 largest corporate R&D budgets, found that innovation *cannot be bought*[7]. The 2006 report did not find any significant statistical relationships between R&D spending and the primary measures of financial or corporate success: sales and earnings growth, gross and operating profitability, market capitalization growth, and total shareholder returns. Gross profits as a percentage of sales is the single performance variable with a statistical relationship to R&D spending. What matters is not the amount spent but how well it is spent. The study found many firms who spent less than their competitors on research and development, yet did better in their industries across a wide range of performance metrics. Booz Allen Hamilton's termed such companies "high-leverage innovators." Companies such as Apple, Toyota, Caterpillar, Black & Decker were all high leverage innovator performers.

Box 1.3: Macro innovation mapping

Although it is not easy to measure the degree of "innovativeness" of an economy, there are some reliable indicators of innovative capacity. One comprehensive study is the annual survey by the OECD, which comes up with the EIS (European Innovation Scoreboard) ranking of European countries. This ranking covers the 25 European Union member states, and a few other countries including the USA and Japan.

The indicators of the EIS summarise the main drivers and outputs of innovation.

(continued)

---

[7] See Jaruzelski et al. (2006).

Box 1.3: Macro innovation mapping (cont.)

These indicators are divided into four groups:
- human resources for innovation (five indicators);
- indicators relating and related to knowledge creation (four indicators);
- indicators relating to transmission and application of knowledge (four indicators);
- finally, a fourth set of indicators relating to innovation finance, output and market (seven indicators).

The figure below shows the innovation scores of selected countries in 2005.

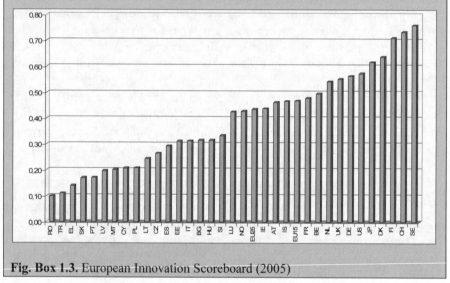

Fig. Box 1.3. European Innovation Scoreboard (2005)

1.3 Classifications

Firms on the innovation path can choose to work from either of two starting points – creating completely new products or services (radical innovation) or they can make improvements on an existing product or service. Although not necessarily the same, incremental improvements of products can lead to product differentiation as well.

The difference between these two starting points is a central theme in research literature on technological innovation, where innovation is broadly divided into either radical or incremental innovation[8]. Radical innovation is thus in the Schumpeterian sense, something that is totally new, in the five areas defined earlier. Incremental innovation generally entails step-by-step improvements of existing products and tends to further strengthen market position.

But categorizing innovation in either of the two camps has not been to the satisfaction of many researchers. It fails to capture the degree of innovation in a product, and hence much research over the last two decades has been devoted to the classification of innovation.

This classification of product innovation has been by and large based along one or both of two dimensions – technology and markets. Abernathy and Clark (1985) for instance categorized four different types of innovation spaces, determined by a market dimension and technological dimension. The market dimension (creating new and/or breaks down existing market linkages vis a vis reinforcing existing market linkages) is mapped against the technological dimension (innovation that makes existing competence obsolete within the technology and production and at the other extreme innovation that reinforces existing competence within technology and production). This gives rise to four different innovation spaces as depicted in Fig.1.2 below. This innovation typology described by the *transilience map* of Abernathy and Clark, was used to describe a product's life cycle.

Further work by Clark, this time with Henderson[9] described another innovation space, where the horizontal axis described the innovation's effect on the existing product's components while the vertical axis symbolizes the innovation's effect on the linkages between the components. This typology described four different product innovations: architectural innovation, incremental innovation, modular innovation and radical innovation. Thus this typology was based on the fact that a product is a sum of its components, the impact of innovation on the links between the components and on the components described the type of innovation.

---

[8] See, in example, Henderson and Clark (1990), Tushman et al. (1997), Chandy and Tellis (1998) and Leifer et al. (2000).
[9] See Henderson and Clark (1990).

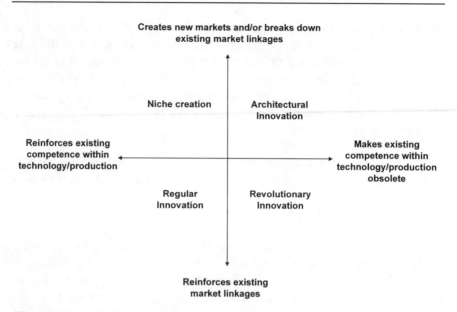

Fig. 1.2. *Transilience map* of Abernathy and Clark (1993)

The creator-user perspective of innovation was proposed by Afuah and Bahram (1995) who argued that it was necessary to view innovation from different perspectives, with regards to different actors. Thus an actor dimension was added which permitted innovation to be also seen in the context of the degree of 'novelty' from the actor perspective.

1.4 So What's New?

Innovation is of course more than creating completely new products or services. In a classic study of innovation published in 1982[10] a survey was undertaken of products considered 'new' between the period 1976 and 1981. Overall 13000 of these 'new' products introduced by 700 firms were surveyed. The study found that there were actually six types of newness, as shown in Table 1.1 below.

---

[10] Booz Allen & Hamilton New Product Management in the 1980s.

Table 1.1. Six types of *newness*

Type	%
New to the world	10
New to the company	20
Line extensions	26
Improvements or revisions	26
Product repositioning	7
Cost reductions	11

Source: Booz Allen & Hamilton (1982)

Thus 90% of products which were considered new and innovative products were really incremental improvements or efficiency gains.

Productscan Online, a consumer products market intelligence firm that studies new product statistics and trend tracking, defines[11] innovation as

> "offering the consumer a significant new or added benefit not offered before."

For a packaged product to be deemed innovative, Productscan Online's Innovation Ratings considers that a product must satisfy at least one of the following six criteria:
- Positioning a product to new users or usage –
- Providing a consumer benefit with new packaging
- Offering additional value through a new formulation
- Introducing new technology to the product
- Opening up a new market for the product
- New merchandising methods to sell the product

Thus while the Schumpeterian view of innovation is maintained in the above criteria, it is more encompassing in that new product usage and new marketing methods are also incorporated when evaluating product innovation. In 2004, *Productscan* found that only 6.2% of food products launched and 7.3% of beverage products launched were innovative!

Hence there are several types of "new" products. Some are new to the firm but not to the market, while others are new to the market and not to the firm and some are new to both. Some involve minor modifications of existing products while some are radical innovations. Fig 1.3 summarizes

---

[11] Source: www.productscan.com

the "newness" of a product along the two dimensions: new to the firm and new to the market.

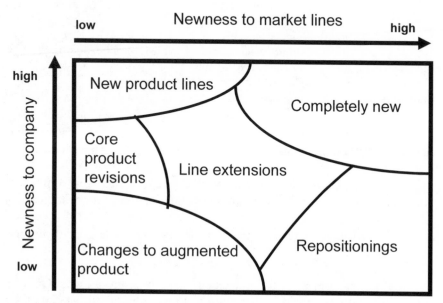

Fig. 1.3. New product types[12]

---

[12] Source: Wikipedia.

Box 1.4: The spread of the weed – diffusion of innovation (cont.)

In a given population the most adventurous were the innovators (2.5%, willing to experiment and with a propensity to risk taking), early adopters (13.5%; are popular and leaders), early majority (34%; who have many informal social contacts), late majority (34%; are sceptic and traditional) and laggards (16%; have fear of debt).

This distribution of consumers is bell shaped and illustrated in the figure below. Rogers then proposes a model of the diffusion of innovation as involving five stages: knowledge (the process of learning the innovation), persuasion (to be convinced), decision (commitment to adopt the innovation), implementation (putting it to use) and confirmation (accepting or rejecting the innovation).

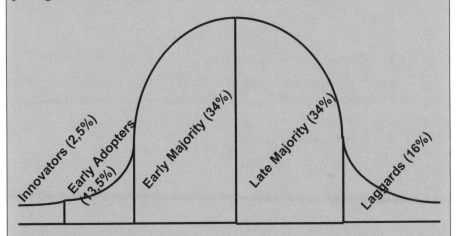

Fig. Box 1.4. Diffusion of innovation

Later, Geoffrey Moore with a focus on high tech products identified that there existed a crucial point- the point between the early adopters and the early majority, which marked the difference between success and failure. Moore called this the *"Crossing the Chasm"* (see Moore, 1999).

2 Innovation and Markets: The Known Paths

No one asks you to throw Mozart out of the
window. Keep Mozart. Cherish him. Keep
Moses too, and Buddha and Lao Tzu and
Christ.
Keep them in your heart. But make room for
the others, the coming ones, the ones who are
already scratching on the window-panes.

The Air-Conditioned Nightmare, *Henry Miller*

2.1 Innovation and Markets

Studying innovation is much like the ancient parable about a group of blind men each touching a different part of an elephant and each satisfied that they understood the true nature of the animal. Innovation literature is vast, both in its scope and depth, with different authors choosing the prudent path of focusing on certain aspects of innovation. The outcome of such focus depends on who the actor is and what the focus is on.

Thus the product manager is more concerned with product innovation, while the CEO is keener to know the outcome of such an innovation, while the finance personnel fret about the costs and uncertain outcome of innovation. The consultant may choose to look at the organizational preparedness for innovation while the economist wonders at the wider implications of new products in the market place. The marketing manager will push for new marketing channels or more effective branding whereas design engineers focus on greater appeal or better usability of the product. All this plays out in an arena in which an economist considers the product to possess basic attributes which have little to differentiate itself from its rivals! Meanwhile the manager in a service sector is busy scratching his head, wondering what innovation in services can possibly mean!

In order to understand the need for an integrated framework that links markets to the outcome of innovation and then to questions on sustainability, it is important to first review briefly how present literature and practice deals with innovation. The following Sects. 2.2 through 2.4 walk us through how markets in industrial organization, strategic management literature and innovation studies deal with various aspects of innovation. This review is not meant to come close to any meaningful literature survey which is beyond the scope of the book, but instead will serve as a brief tour of some principal strands of thought dealing with innovation in the context of markets and market structures. This review then enables us to put the Integrated Innovation Model in context.

2.2 Innovation Through the Lens of: Industrial Organization

In economics students learn of the different types of markets, namely competitive markets, monopolistic competition, oligopoly and monopoly. Each of these market structures are characterized by a set of behavioural assumptions, such as the ease of entry and exit into the industry, the number of firms existing, degree of homogeneity of the product etc. Although the literature is rich (see Tirole, 1988) in the many strategic variables of firms (all quantifiable), price is generally considered to be the most important strategic tool for profit maximizing firms. Thus the strategic variable of choice in each market is the price (or its inverse, quantity). To put it simply, what characterizes each market in the industrial organization literature is the degree of freedom a firm has in that market to set its own price.

The study of industrial organization is largely an analysis of optimal pricing of firms given a set of behavioural conditions and market characteristics. At the optimum, the price of a firm's product is given by the relationship, $MC = P(1 - 1/e)$ where e is own price elasticity and MC is the marginal cost of the firm. This relationship is derived from the *golden rule* of profit maximization which states that maximum profit occurs at a point where marginal cost equals marginal revenue. Markets are then classified according to the degree of competition (which determines the own price elasticity).

Fig. 2.1 summarises the market structures and some of the different strategy variables generally considered in the literature of industrial organisation. Product differentiation in economics refers to:

> "Such variations within a product class that (some) consumers view as imperfect substitutes[1]."

Product differentiation enables firms to escape from the gravitational force of marginal cost pricing allowing firms to charge a premium over costs[2]. Frequently differentiation is introduced in the models usually via space (where space is used as a metaphor for product differentiation) or via different demand elasticities (see Box 2.1).

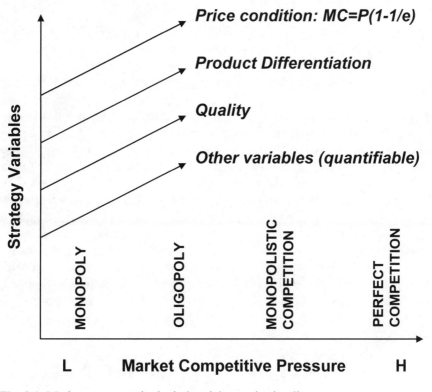

Fig. 2.1. Market structures in the industrial organisation literature

---

[1] Simon P. Anderson: entry in the New Palgrave Dictionary.
[2] Sometimes referred to as the Bertrand Paradox in economics, if consumers perceive two goods as being identical, and then assuming that marginal costs were same and constant, then marginal cost pricing would be the only equilibrium.

Box 2.1: Space as product differentiator

In the spatial literature of product differentiation space is used as a metaphor. Each spatial dimension represents a given characteristic of the product and a point in space represents a given combination of the various characteristics. In this product space one can represent the products offered by the various firms (each product has certain values of the various characteristics, thus it can be represented by a point in the product space). Typically firms will offer products with different characteristics' values, thus spatial models are used to study product differentiation. A consumer location is defined by her ideal product in this space. The utility each consumer gets with a given product depends on how distant that product is from the consumer's ideal product.

This artifice was first introduced by Hotelling (1929), with his famous "linear city model" which goes something like this.

Assume consumers to be uniformly distributed along a linear city of length 1. There are two stores (firms) located at the two extremes of the city, which sell the same physical product. Consumers incur a transportation cost which depends on their distance from each firm. Thus the generalized price paid by the consumer equals the price plus the transportation cost. As long as the generalized price is below the consumer's reservation price she would buy from the firm with the lowest generalized price. The demand of each firm is given by the set of consumers who find it cheaper to buy from that firm, which depends on the prices of both firms and on the transportation costs. Given demands one can derive the equilibrium prices. For a given rival's price, each firm chooses its price so as to maximize profit. Equilibrium prices are above marginal costs and increase with transportation costs (which can be interpreted as the differentiation degree). The model can also be used to study the product differentiation decision, by considering a first stage where firms choose their location in the line.

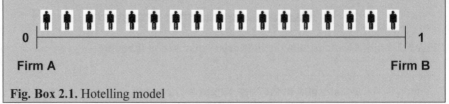

Firm A   **Firm B**

Fig. Box 2.1. Hotelling model

As had been mentioned earlier, each of the markets in economics is characterised by a set of behavioural assumptions. For instance in perfectly competitive markets, a product is assumed to be homogenous with a large number of buyers and sellers who individually have little market power, with free entry and exit of firms. The implication of this is that a seller in a perfectly competitive market acts as a price taker. Thus, in each of the other market archetypes, there are market characteristics, which determine the degree of market power of a firm.

Studies in the neoclassical economic vein have attempted to show how innovation is connected to growth and other studies focused on innovation decision theory. Using game theory, Dasgupta and Stiglitz for instance attempt to identify *"which market structure will lead to optimal scope for R&D from macroeconomic viewpoint."*

2.3 Innovation in Strategy Literature

In management literature, specifically in management strategy, there are a plethora of relatively simple and intuitive models for both managers and consultants to choose from. Most of these models provide insights to the manager which help in crafting a strategic plan consistent with the desired aims. Indeed most strategy models are generally simple, wherein lie their virtue.

Over the years, academics and consultants have devised their own models to enable firms to see the *where* (firms are situated) to prepare them to devise methods to achieve their objectives and foresee coming changes for them to adapt and evolve. Among the many models are - the PEST analysis, the five competitive forces, value chain analysis, McKinsey seven S analysis, the driving forces analysis, the Ansoff matrix, the BCG growth-share matrix, Porter's Generic Strategies, and the Space Matrix (Have et al., 2003). More recently Tesmer (2002), has come up with an archetypal model, which tries to match organisations with market environments.

Given the conceptual approach of most of these models, strategy model rarely deal with innovation as an explicit variable. However innovation or new products or markets is often built into some of the models as a dimension. Geared towards helping the manager devise competitive strategies, the 2x2 conceptual matrices are designed to help the firm understand firm and market position along the dimensions chosen by a particular model.

Box 2.2: An innovation strategy model

Arguably, a representative example of a widely used model in management strategy is the Ansoff matrix. Also called the "Product/market expansion grid" of Ansoff (1957), it is a model, despite whose half a century of existence remains popular in business unit strategy processes to determine business growth opportunities. Two dimensions determine the scope of options, *products* and *markets*.

The Ansoff framework permits analyses of four generic growth strategies:

1. **Market Penetration**. Sell more of the same products or services in the current market-product combination. Strategy is often to realize economies of scale via increase in the efficiency of manufacturing, distribution, more purchasing power or overhead sharing.

2. **Market Development**. This strategy refers to selling more of existing products or services in new markets or channels. These strategies imply enticing clients away from competitors or introducing new brand names in a market. New markets can also be explored internationally.

3. **Product Development**. This refers to the development of new products to replace or complement current products. The focus is on product development to regular clients.

4. **Diversification**. This space refers to selling new products or services in new markets. Diversification strategies can either increase (due to newness) or reduce risks (by spreading risks) Within the. diversification space, four growth vectors can be identified:

   - *Horizontal diversification* – acquiring or developing new products introduced in the current consumer groups

   - *Vertical diversification* – moving into the suppliers or consumers business to secure supply or strengthen consumption.

   - *Concentric diversification* – introduction of new product lines or services closely related to existing product lines, to new consumer groups.

   - *Conglomerate diversification* – introduction of products that are completely new technological unrelated and reaching new customer groups.

(continued)

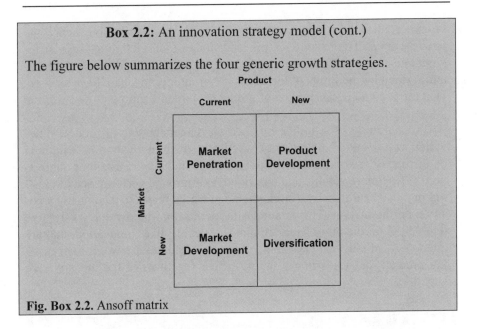

Box 2.2: An innovation strategy model (cont.)

The figure below summarizes the four generic growth strategies.

Fig. Box 2.2. Ansoff matrix

2.4 Innovation Literature

In the previous section we saw some definitions and classifications of innovation. Innovation literature has been enriched along other dimensions as well, mostly on the dynamics of the innovation process described by the product life cycle. The idea of a product lifecycle in technological innovation research was articulated by Abernathy and Utterback (1978) who noted that the nature of innovation around a product could vary during its life time. The product life cycle trajectory begins with the emergence of a new product characterized by experimentation and learning about and by users and then the subsequent stages of the life cycle is based upon the economics of innovation, from novelty products to mass production and commoditization. The transition from novelty products to mass production is marked by the emergence of a dominant design.

The technology life cycle is also described by an S-Curve when the product reaches its technical evolution towards a physical limit[3]. The diffusion of the product follows a similar pattern. Given appropriate simplifying assumptions both technical progress and market diffusion through time can

---

[3] See Foster (1986).

be expected to approximate a cumulative logistic distribution (hence the term S-curve). The technology proceeds up an S-curve through regular innovation[4]. As it proceeds up that S-curve, it diffuses to fill the market circumscribed by the limits of the needs it can satisfy. In Chap. 8 we shall revisit the S-curve in the context of product commoditization.

Christensen (1997) further enriched our understanding of product innovation as a result of his query of whether a given innovation is sustaining or disruptive to established firms in a given industry. Sustaining innovations refer to innovations that contribute to improved performance of existing products and thereby a strengthening of each respective company's position on the market. This is similar to incremental innovation. Disruptive innovation on the other hand are almost 'stealth' like innovation, that are due to new products at least some of whose attributes are worse than existing product, but leads to the failure of leading firms in the industry (see Box 2.3).

Box 2.3: Disruptive innovation

Clayton Christensen (1997) coined the phrase "disruptive technologies" a term which has since caught on and is widely used (often incorrectly, if one is to stick to the author's original description) when discussing the emergence of new technologies or products. His original research was on the disk drive industry.

Established firms focusing attention and investment on their principal clients or markets, as they are supposed to do, are on a path of sustaining innovations. Sustaining innovations can be simple, incremental, year-to-year improvements or sometimes can mark dramatic technological breakthroughs: However the overwhelming focus on existing customers or proven market segments can leave incumbent firms vulnerable to new disruptive technologies. Disruptive innovations are typically cheaper and simpler to use versions of existing products that target less demanding or entirely new customers.

(continued)

---

[4] Idem.

Box 2.3: Disruptive innovation (cont.)

Once the new firm, the 'disruptor' has gained foot hold in this customer segment, it then moves along its own sustaining innovation trajectory. Meanwhile, typically the incumbent will move up market, over serving its customers. As we can see from the figure, the disruptor as it focuses on improvements in its own product has very soon entered into the mainstream market, driving the established company out of the market.

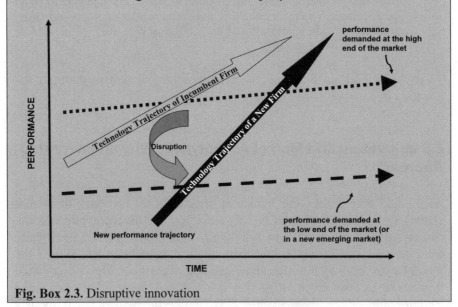

Fig. Box 2.3. Disruptive innovation

From our quick tour through the innovation literature landscape both in the previous chapter and in this section, it is evident that most of the research over the years has focussed on trying to understand the innovation process and its dynamics. As a result its companion, innovation typology, is often filled with a plethora of different innovation types e.g., incremental, regular, continuous, modular, architectural, evolutionary, revolutionary, really new, breakthrough, discontinuous, and radical innovations. This richness has led academics to achieve a better understanding of product innovation. Yet at the same time, both these myriad definitions as well as the dynamics of product innovation, (almost all from a product-technology perspective) have often muddied the waters for those wishing to understand innovation from more holistic perspectives. This is especially true when it comes to trying to understand the relationship between innovation and market outcome. Indeed one can often get lost in the muddling array of classifications, terminologies, measures, sources etc. Indeed this was sharply brought to attention by the authors Gatignon, Tushman, Anderson and Smith, when they noted that[5]:

> "...after more than 30 years of research on innovation and organizational outcomes, fundamental concepts and units of analysis remain confused and ambiguous....The innovation literature is littered with concepts that are inconsistently defined and conceptually confused. Given this conceptual confusion, innovation research confounds innovation characteristics, innovation types and the hierarchical locus of the innovation. With greater clarity on units of analysis and on innovation concepts and measures, research on innovation and organizational outcomes might be more cumulative and impactful."

All this obliges us to address the need for a holistic understanding of innovation in a market based framework.

2.5 Innovation and Market Archetypes: Why an Integrated Approach?

As we had seen earlier, the industrial organizational approach of market characterization according to the degree of competitive pressure and the consequent modelling of firm behaviour often using sophisticated game theoretic tools, while permitting mathematical modelling, has shifted the ground away from an intuitive understanding of markets. The earlier visual framework in economics, of market demand and supply along price and quantity dimensions, has given way to powerful mathematical models which though intellectually satisfying has led policy makers and managers groping for more intuitive and less theoretical analyses to which they can relate to at a practical level. Non quantifiable variables find little place in these models, and when they do, mathematical gymnastics (such as the use of different demand elasticities for differentiated products) embrace many of these qualitative variables, but in an intuitively unsatisfactory way.

In the management (strategy) literature on the other hand, there is a vast array of relatively simple and intuitive models for both managers and consultants to choose from. Most of these models provide insights to the manager which help in crafting a strategic plan consistent with the desired aims. Indeed most strategy models are generally simple, wherein lie their virtue. In the process however, these models often fail to offer insights into

---

[5] See Gatignon et al. (2002).

situations beyond that for which they are designed, often due to the adoption of frameworks seldom analytical, seldom rigorous. The situational analyses of these models often tend to be descriptive and seldom robust and rarely present behavioural relationship between variables under study. Take the BCG model for instance, useful for determining priorities in the product portfolio of an organization. The product offering is characterized by its position determined by two variables – market share and market growth. A position once determined is then subject to descriptive analyses where the knowledge and experience of the analyst, often a consultant, come to play. No underlying theoretical relationship between variables is posited and consequently no intellectually meaningful dynamic analyses can be performed. This is not to detract from the role of this or any other models for their virtue lie in their practical approach to situation analyses for strategy design.

From an academic point of view, there is often a divorce between industrial organisation theory and strategic management models. While many economists view management models as being too simplistic, strategic management consultants perceive academic economists as being too theoretical, and the analytical tools that they devise as too complex for managers to understand.

Innovation literature, some of whose main strands were described earlier, while rich in typologies and descriptions of innovation dynamics is mostly technology focused. As mentioned before, most research on innovation has been devoted to the process (technological) of innovation, or has otherwise taken a *how to* (innovate) approach. There remains a strong need for the academic, the manager and the consultant to have an intuitive understanding of the innovation – market linkages in a simple yet rigorous framework. There is also a need for a holistic understanding of innovation, which link both external environmental factors to strategic decisions. The Integrated Model that we present in the next chapter is intended precisely to fill such a gap.

The book is organised as follows. Chaps. 1 and 2 provided the backdrop for understanding the context of the Integrated Innovation Model. We reviewed in Chap. 1 some major definitions of innovation and further explored the concept as well as major classifications of innovation. And in this chapter (Chap.2) we discussed how markets in industrial organization, strategic management literature and innovation studies dealt with various aspects of innovation. This review then enables us to put the Integrated Innovation Model in context which is discussed in the next chapter.

Chap. 3 provides the framework applied for much of the remainder of the book. An *integrated innovation space* is presented in the form of a four quadrant graphical model. This integrated spaces allows us to map *where* a product (single product firm) is located, *why* it is so located which then provides valuable clues as to *what* to do while designing strategy.

Chap. 4 examines the archetype space, one of the four spaces described by the Integrated Model In this space we describe four major market archetypes characterised by the differences in their competitive market pressure and the degree of product differentiation. Characteristics of each of the four archetypes are described along with examples. The chapter also presents a *radiograph* of the major characteristics of each of the archetypes.

Chap. 5 delves into market dynamics, both internal (strategic moves of innovation and product differentiation) as well as external (changes in the environment). The simplicity afforded by the visual framework as well as the internal rigor of the model is very useful because, to explain several market evolutions - the impact of increased competition, the product life cycle, the innovation struggle for maintaining market position, the sustainability of the innovation or the disruptive innovation, among others. These dynamics are studied in this chapter.

Chap. 6 focuses on one of the most important aspect of innovation: how can innovation be sustained? What are the factors behind sustainability of market leaders? This is explained using a real example of the continuous effort at incremental innovative of a single highly successful product - the Apple iPod. The innovation efforts are mapped on the integrated innovation space, and two dimensions are used for the first time - market shares and margins marking the iPod generational trail.

Chap. 7 illustrates three cases of the constant striving to stay relevant in a turbulent market space. Two of the cases are in the toy industry (LEGO and Barbie) and the third in the browser industry. The case of the LEGO building bricks point to how, long established leaders now have to constantly innovate to stay relevant. The case of Barbie is even more pressing in that besides trying to stay relevant, she has to contend with a director competitor. The third case is about the browser war and we follow the dramatic rise and fall of Netscape with the accompanying rise of Microsoft's Internet Explorer. All three cases are illustrated by the Integrated Model.

In Chap. 8 we study the omnipresent threat of commoditization The shrinking life span of a product with the impending prospect of commoditization in the not too distant future, and accelerated obsolescence of even very innovative products is explored at some depth in this chapter. We begin with an understanding of both the life cycle of a product as well as the technology life cycle. The emergence of a dominant industrial design is discussed to better understand the commoditization process. Finally we explain commoditization in the integrated innovation space.

Chap. 9 surveys the apparent escape from the commoditization trap in the case of search engines in general and Google in particular. The chapter focuses on the attempts at differentiation by search engines (with the integrated innovation space forming the backdrop) which hold interesting insights into the differentiation strategies employed.

Chap. 10 elaborates on the diagnostic matrix and how firms can benefit from an understanding of their position in the integrated environment – internal, external and organizational, relative to the market and the market leaders. The chapter first discusses some of the firm level diagnostics used and also macro innovation measures. The survey associated with internal diagnostic is divided into three parts, one for each dimension of the model- the degree of competitive market, the degree of innovation/differentiation and market results. Internal diagnostics map - the locus of a product, perform cluster mapping (product position with respect to the industry and the leader) and enable intrafirm-gap mapping, which permits the manager to detect mismatches in variables in any dimension.

While innovation diagnostics permitted by the model can serve as an important tool for the manager, we have so far eschewed from dwelling on management strategy as relates to innovation. In Chap. 11 we discuss some issues relating to innovation strategy. This chapter is meant to give a broad sweep of the innovation landscape from the strategy perspective. The chapter first presents some important survey results on how CEOs view the innovation horizon. The chapter then discusses two fundamental strategy related issues with regards to innovation and market outcome - *innovation payoff*, and *"Organovate"* – having an innovation ready organization.

Box 2.4: Innovation in the service sector

The economic growth of the last two decades is strongly driven by the service sector development, in which the role of. Information and communication technologies (ICT) have been fundamental. Given the importance of the service sector as the largest productive sector in developed economies, it is increasingly important to understand the innovation process in services.

The diversity of activities included in the service sector makes it difficult even to define. Services initially were classified as non-productive activities. As quoted by Hauknes (1999) one characterises services as "anything sold in trade that could not be dropped on your foot!"

In general, studying the service sector is fairly complicated, more so with regards to innovation. Most models and research on the innovation process were studies with the manufacturing sector in mind. In the table below, we summarize three contributions towards defining innovation in services.

Table Box 2.4. Innovation in services

Definition	Source
Service innovations are often small adjustments of procedures and thus incremental and rarely radical. The development time for service innovation is generally relatively short since there is need for research or collection of scientific knowledge. Services innovation processes are normally very practical	Sundbo and Gallouj (1999) p.9
Service innovation is by definition multidimensional. Compared to, for instance manufacturing, service innovation is characterized by much greater emphasis on the organizational dimension of innovation (new service concepts, new client interface and new delivery systems) relative the technological options	Van Ark et al (2003), p.5
The introduction of significantly new products and services or implementations of significantly improved process	Licht, et al (1999) p.6

3 Innovation: An Integrated Framework

All things appear and disappear
because of the concurrence of causes and conditions.
Nothing ever exists entirely alone
everything is in relation to everything else.

Attributed to *the Buddha*, 563–483 BC

3.1 What Is the Integrated Approach?

The integrated framework of innovation[1] is a market based approach for understanding innovation, its (market) outcome dynamics and product life cycle, enriched by our understanding of three (mutually non exclusive) fields of study – industrial organization, strategy and innovation.

As we have seen in the previous chapter, the industrial organizational approach of market characterization has shifted the ground away from an intuitive understanding of markets, with the visual framework, of market demand and supply giving way to powerful mathematical models. These models while intellectually satisfying and mathematically rich, has led policy makers and managers groping for more intuitive and less theoretical analyses to which they can relate to at a practical level. Non quantifiable variables find little place in these models.

The literature on management (strategy) offers a wide array of relatively simple and intuitive models of strategy (as well as organizational management). Most of these models provide insights to designing effective strategy, and their virtue often lies in their simplicity and intuitive appeal (when free of jargon!). In the process however, these models are seldom analytical or robust, lacking in any behavioural relationship between variables under study.

---

[1] An earlier version of the model was first published in 2005 by this author. See Sarkar (2005).

Innovation literature, some of whose main strands were described in the earlier chapters, while rich in typologies and descriptions of innovation dynamics, is mostly technology focused. As our previous brief tour revealed, most research on innovation has been devoted to definitions, the processes (technological) and classifications of innovation. Consultants have focused on a *how to* (innovate) approach.

The Integrated Innovation Model is meant to fill a huge gap in the understanding of innovation to market linkages, sustainability and outcomes in an intuitive yet rigorous framework. It is a new framework for understanding firm and market dynamics, as it relates to innovation. The model is enriched by the different strands of literature - industrial organization, management and innovation. Ours is an integrated approach that allows the academic, the management consultant and the manager alike to understand *where* a product (or a single product firm) is located in **an integrated innovation space**, *why* it is so located and which then provides valuable clues as to *what* to do while designing strategy. We believe that the integration of the important determinant variables in one visual framework with a robust and an internally consistent theoretical basis is an important step towards devising comprehensive firm strategy. The integrated framework provides vital clues towards framing a *what to* guide for managers and consultants. Furthermore, the model permits *metrics* and consequently *diagnostics* of both the firm and the sector and this set of assessment tools provide a valuable guide for devising strategy.

In the following chapters we present the Integrated Model, which has two frameworks: an *analytical framework* where the model is presented, innovation and market dynamics explained and a *diagnostic framework* where the model is put to an empirical application. The diagnostic test was designed with a total of thirty questions with a further set of diagnostics of the organizational culture of the firm.

Box 3.1 below highlights the different dimensions, the issues explored and some of the questions answered in both the *analytical* and the *diagnostic framework* of the Integrated Model.

Box 3.1: An x-ray of the integrated approach

The multiplicity of terms used is a natural consequence of the vastness of the topic under study, all within a single framework. It is helpful however to summarize the major issues at the outset- the dimensions understudy, frameworks used, model objectives and a sample of questions answered. However the author believes that the model is still in its infancy in terms of the applications that it can be put to, and the questions that the model permits analyses of.

1. Dimensions:
- Market (competitive pressure)
- Strategic (choice) variable
- Outcome(s)

2. Framework:
- Analytical
- Diagnostic

3. What it enables:
- Explains product positioning (market archetypes)
- An integration between market competition, strategic orientation and market outcome
- Explains various innovation-market dynamics (analytical framework)
- Enables firm level diagnostics and benchmarking (diagnostic matrix)

4. Some of the issues explored and questions answered using the analytical matrix:
- Studies market returns from innovation.
- Relationship between, market competition, product differentiation and market returns.
- Relationship between two types of market returns (for instance market share- margins)
- Explaining product life cycle and different dynamics of (ever shortening product life cycle)
- Explores the issue of sustainability of innovation
- Explores some dynamics of disruptive innovation

(continued)

Box 3.1: An x-ray of the integrated approach (cont.)

4. Some of the issues explored and questions answered using the analytical matrix (cont.):
- Explains different `why`'s! For instance:
    - Why do two firms which face similar market pressure yet have very different market outcomes
    - Why is it that two firms can have similar market share but different profit margins
        - Why do firms need to innovate to stay ahead

5. And what the diagnostics matrix permits:
- Enables firms to ´see´ their position in the model, in terms of external, strategic and outcome.
- Enables a benchmark of firms, along different dimension, against market leaders
    - Diagnosis of mismatch within variables in the same dimension
    - Diagnosis of mismatch between organizational culture and market position
    - Enables design of a comprehensive strategy
    - Provides forecasting tools

Besides these four dimensions of the model, there are other variables that impinge upon a firm's position in the integrated innovation space. These variables include *price, market size and market growth, productivity, factor costs, marketing and profit margins.*

In the current chapter we describe the Integrated Innovation Model. Sect. 3.2 presents the basic framework and Sect. 3.3 explains the Integrated (Innovation) Model.

3.2 The Integrated Model: the Basic Framework

The model describes a product[2] (or a single product firm) along four dimensions[3] - an external market dimension, a dimension on the strategic orientation, and two outcome dimensions. These four dimensions together define four spaces: *an archetype space, a strategy space, an outcome*

---

[2] The model explains and maps the position of either a product or a single product firm in the integrated space. References to a firm in the model are of a single product firm.

[3] See Box 3.2 for a definition and explanation of our choice of terminology.

space and a market space. These four spaces in concert describe the *integrated innovation space.*

1. **Archetype Space**: A product (or a single product firm) is situated in an archetype space determined by two dimensions: an external (market) and an internal (strategic) dimension. The external market dimension, is a *given* to the firm, and is the competitive market pressure that it faces. The second dimension is a strategic orientation variable, which is represented by the degree of innovation-product differentiation.

Situational Analysis: The location of a product in the archetype space describes the following:
- What (how innovative/differentiated) is your product?
- How competitive is the marketplace you are in?
- To whom are you selling?

In the next chapter we describe in detail four product or market archetypes in this space.

2. **The Strategy Space**: The second of our four spaces, positions a product or a single product firm in terms of its strategic orientation (innovation/product differentiation) and the resulting market outcome. These two variables are connected via a behavioural relationship.

3. **The Outcome Space**: In the outcome space we trace out the relationship between two market outcome variables. The *outcome space* is the outcome of the firm's strategic positioning. Later on we explain the market outcome variables as sales, market share or profits, the two being connected via a behavioural relationship.

4. **The Market Space**: This space defines the competitive pressure faced by the product and the market outcome. The market outcome of a firm as we shall show, is related to its strategic orientation.

Situational Analysis: The location of a product in the market space describes the following:
- How competitive is the marketplace?
- How comfortable are your margins?

The *visual representation of the model is a four quadrant matrix* that positions a product (single product firm) in terms of its external market dimension, its strategic positioning and market outcome. **The four spaces corresponding to the four quadrants unite in a single analytical framework** that we call the **integrated space,** and when the strategic choice variable is innovation (Sec.3.3), this space is then the **integrated innovation space.**

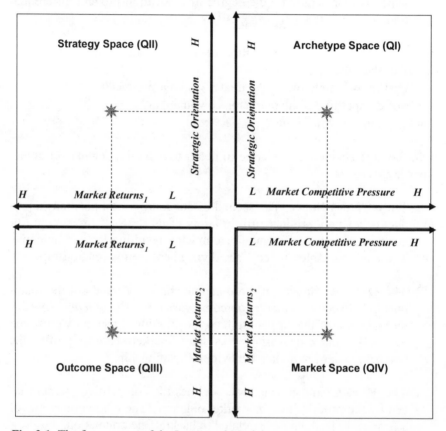

Fig. 3.1. The four spaces of the Integrated Model

Fig. 3.1 presents the four different dimensions and associated environments in the Integrated Model.

Box 3.2: A word about our choice of terminology

Aside from the use of imaginative metaphors in management and popular business literature (a temptation to which we too succumb), there is a bewildering number of references and usage of words such as spaces, environment, dimensions etc, used in different contexts and with different interpretations. A Google search for instance came up with around 60 million references to the phrase 'consumer space' and almost twice that many references to the phrase 'market space'. The interpretation of these phrases is contextual and is often fuzzy and ambiguous with the phrases rarely defined. However on closer inspection many of these phrases reveal fundamentally simple, known expressions and behaviours, cloaked in 'management speak'!

We make every attempt to be careful with terminology, although this is not easy given our desire to introduce the many different variables and dynamics into one model that come to play in the actual business environment. *Dimension* for instance is used in the mathematical and geometrical sense - a measure of spatial extent. Although space is in three dimensions, adoption of this term is for each of the four axes, as a dimension, where variables (market pressure, strategic orientation and outcome(s)) are measured. Every two adjacent 'dimensions' in our model describe a *space*. Given our four quadrant model, each quadrant therefore describes a space. The first is the archetype space which describes a product (or a single product firm) according to the degree of market pressure and its degree of differentiation. The second quadrant is the strategy space which gives the relationship between strategic orientation and outcome. The third quadrant describes the relationship between two outcome measures (outcome space). The fourth quadrant gives the relationship between market pressure and outcome (market space). We often interchange the word space, which is often static in its connotation with 'environment'. The space described by the model is the *integrated space.*

Analyses can either be for a product or single product firms (or groups thereof). *Market returns* and *market outcomes* are used interchangeably, although the use of the term 'market returns' is made when specific measurable outcome is in mind, (such as market share, sales, profits or profit margins), whereas market outcome can include other variables such as consumer satisfaction.

(continued)

Box 3.2: A word about our choice of terminology (cont.)

Finally: is it a model, a framework? In addition to our general choice and usage of the word 'model', we often also use the word 'framework' given the visual structure of the model. Nevertheless, it remains a 'model' where we describe a systematic process in a system with a set of variables and behavioural relationships between them.

Besides the four dimensions of the model, there are other variables that impinge on a firm's position in the integrated innovation space. These variables include price, market size and market growth, productivity, factor costs, marketing and profit margins. With regards to a particular positioning of the firm, these factors appear as parameters, hence changes in these variables would affect the firm positioning in the integrated space.

3.3 The Integrated Model of Innovation

Having described our basic framework, let us now take a closer inspection of the integrated space described by the model and the key role of innovation in determining market outcome, competitiveness and firm growth. As seen earlier, the visual representation of the model is a four quadrant framework, numbered I through IV, moving anti-clockwise as in Fig. 3.1, where each quadrant corresponds to one of the four spaces defined in the preceding section.

In the first and north-east quadrant which describes the *archetype space*, (Fig. 3.1), the external market dimension in which a firm operates is represented by the degree of competitive market pressure on the horizontal axis. A product or firms located further to the right are under increasing competitive pressure often represented by an increase in the number of firms in the industry[4]. In Chap. 10 where we present the diagnostics framework, we explain how our metrics enable us measure competitive pressure using a mix of different variables. Drawing a parallel to economic theory, moving along horizontally to the right on the competitive pressure axis implies a decrease in the freedom for the firm in setting the price. Thus own price

---

[4] Although we speak of industry and product, our analyses also include firms in the service industry. The degree of competition is often, but not necessarily, positively correlated to the number of firms. A few firms in an industry can lead to strong competitive pressures if they follow for instance, Bertrand type conjectures.

elasticity of demand increases, in absolute terms, with an increase in the competitive pressure[5].

The vertical axis in the archetype space measures a firm's strategic orientation. In the innovation context (of the general framework), the strategic orientation is an innovation-product differentiation strategy. When we describe market archetypes in Chap. 4, we explain in further detail when we consider a strategy to be one of innovation and when of differentiation. Note too that other than improvements in product characteristics, such as branding, after sales services, bundling, pricing strategy can all help at least for the short term, in creating a differentiation strategy[6].

Moving anti-clockwise, the *strategy space* gives the trade off between a firm's strategic orientation and market return. While the archetype space describes a firm according to the coordinates of an external (market)-internal (strategic) relationship, the strategy space defines its market outcome with respect to its strategic orientation. The second quadrant therefore describes a strategy space where the two variables innovation and market outcome are connected via a behavioural relationship.

The market outcome of the firm in its competitive environment can be variously represented by a variable such as sales, market share, margins or profits[7], with a westward or outward movement away from the origin representing an increased level of market share (or other outcome variable). We suggest a generic pay-off function represented by upward sloping,

---

[5] In chap. 2 earlier, we had mentioned the profit maximizing rule, with a profit maximizing firm charging a price which depends not only on the marginal production cost but the own price elasticity of demand. The greater the market competition, the greater (in absolute terms) is own price elasticity. Thus in perfectly competitive markets (products located to the very right of the archetype space) have very high own price elasticities (infinity), with demand curves being horizontal. These firms act as price takers. At the other end (regions to the left of the archetype space), firms are price makers, with own price elasticity being zero or close to. Demand curves are vertical in this case.

[6] Industrial economics and micro economic theory often deal with differentiation in the spatial or temporal sense, as we mentioned in chap. 2. Our model deals explicitly with product or service differentiation. Thus while there are a number of elements which all together define the strategic orientation of a firm in a particular market environment, these elements of strategic orientation depend upon the specific industry under study.

[7] In some cases we explicitly work with two market outcome variables, with a behavioural relationship between the two in the third quadrant. See also Box 3.3.

concave surfaces. These curves represent *the return from activities associated with a given degree of market pressure, between the strategic orientation pursued and the outcome of that strategy.* We posit a positive relationship between the strategic orientation (innovation/product differentiation) and the resulting market share in the industry. We call these curves the *innovation – pay-off (IP) curves.* The exact curvature or elasticity of these IP functions is industry specific. These IP curves, associated with a given degree of market pressure, can shift either temporally due to different factors including evolving product and labour market conditions, technological changes and (disruptive) innovation. Fig. 3.2 illustrates two IP curves *each associated with different market or competitive environments.* Curve **I'-I'** reflects the pay-off from greater product differentiation in a market with lower competitive pressure, while **I-I** gives the pay-off in a market characterised by greater market pressure. In terms of innovation, movement up along the curve represents incremental or sustaining innovation.

Hence coordinates of a product in the strategy space give the market outcome enjoyed by the firm in a given competitive environment that is the result of the degree of innovation or product differentiation pursued. Ceteris paribus, a higher level of product differentiation by a firm would lead to an increase in market outcome (sales, market share or profits). Fig. 3.2 below illustrates the case of our different products in two different market environments (small and large market pressure) and with two different innovation payoff curves.

Products (or single product firms) **2** and **3** operate in markets characterised by low competitive pressure as opposed to firms **1** and **4** which are in more competitive markets. Although in the same market environment, firm **1** pursues a strategy of a greater degree of product differentiation than **4**. The same holds true for the less competitive market, where firm **2** is more innovative than **3**. Market returns of firm **2** are the highest, due to offering an innovative product in a market environment characterised by little competition as well as a payoff curve that lies further out (due to the lesser degree of market pressure). On the other hand, firm **3**, in a similarly less competitive environment as **2** has lower market returns due to the lower degree of innovation. Indeed, the returns of firm **3**, in our example are lower than a firm which is under more competitive pressure, but which pursues a higher degree of product differentiation, like firm **1** in the illustration. It is perhaps important to draw attention to the fact that moving up along an IP curve involves resources either financial and/or, a combination of measures which include cost cutting and productivity enhancement.

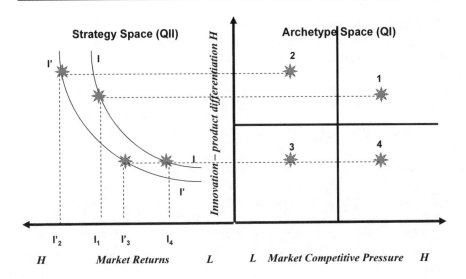

Fig. 3.2. Archetype and strategy space

The third quadrant describes the *outcome space*, but in an effort to keep the model simple, we choose only one variable to represent firm outcome given its strategic orientation (innovation strategy). This space maps market outcome measured by sales, market share or profits, on to itself via the 45° line. This device enables us to study in the final southeast quadrant, the correspondence between returns and competitive pressure. Later on in this outcome space, we shall describe a behavioural relationship between two important market outcome variables, market share and profits.

The fourth quadrant maps the external environment to market returns for a given strategic orientation (innovation). We call this space the *market space*, which locates the market outcome for a given degree of competitive pressure. The market outcome of the product (single product firm), is in turn related to the degree of product innovation/differentiation via the integration of the strategic space and the outcome space.

Fig. 3.3 presents our Integrated Model as a four quadrant graphical framework. In the first quadrant, the archetype space, we have the product-market environment given by the market pressure and the degree of innovation-product differentiation. The second quadrant locates the market outcome as a result of the innovation-product differentiation strategy employed. This is the strategy space. The third quadrant employs the 45° line that enables us to study in the fourth quadrant the market environment, which gives the relationship between market outcome and the market competitive environment for a given degree of innovation or product differentiation. Before we look at the market environment let us see some illustrations of the Integrated Model as in Fig. 3.3.

Box 3.3: The *Outcome Space* with two different variables

As a general case and for the sake of simplicity, the integrated innovation model, as in fig. 3.3, uses one outcome variable in the outcome space. This outcome variable chosen can be - sales, market share, margins or profits However, when there is a need for more complete analyses the outcome space can incorporate two distinct variables, for instance market share and profits. These two variables are interrelated via a behavioural relationship such as a generic concave curve as shown in the figure below. This implies that an increase in market share would increase profits at a diminishing rate.

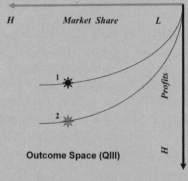

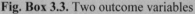

Fig. Box 3.3. Two outcome variables

Explicitly introducing two outcome variables permits a richer analysis of firm diagnostics. For instance it permits an understanding of why firms with equal market shares may have different profits (**1** and **2**). We can thus analyse cases involving similar market pressures and product differentiation but different outcomes. Changes in factors such as price, market size and market growth, productivity, factor costs, marketing or profit margins would cause corresponding shifts of the curve relating the two outcome variables. All this permits more complete and richer dynamic analyses of innovation and market outcome.

Fig. 3.3 below illustrates the case of two firms **1** and **2**. Firm **1** faces a fairly competitive environment and in its effort to stand above the crowd, offers a more differentiated product.

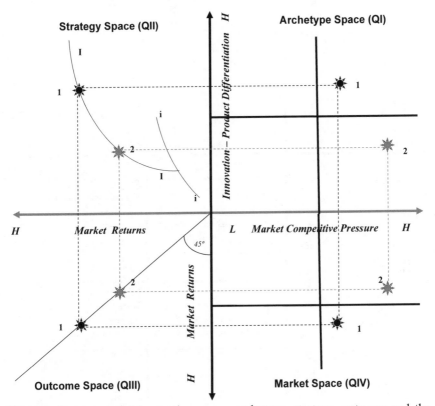

Fig. 3.3. The integrated innovation space: archetype, strategy, outcome and the market space

The framework traces out the resulting market outcome given the degree of its product differentiation. In the fourth quadrant we can see the result of its differentiation strategy in its competitive environment by the market outcome it enjoys. In contrast the second firm (firm **2**) has been unable to offer a differentiated product in the high competitive environment it faces. This reflects in the low market outcome (in terms of sales, market share or profits) as reflected in the fourth quadrant.

In reality of course the IP curves should be different, where the IP curve of firm **2** is more inward and consequently with an even smaller market share. This is suggested by the IP curve of firm **2**, as given by **I'-I'** in the strategy space. We have chosen to keep the figure as simple as possible but it obvious that in the same competitive environment and low differentiation offering, firm **2** has an even much smaller market outcome.

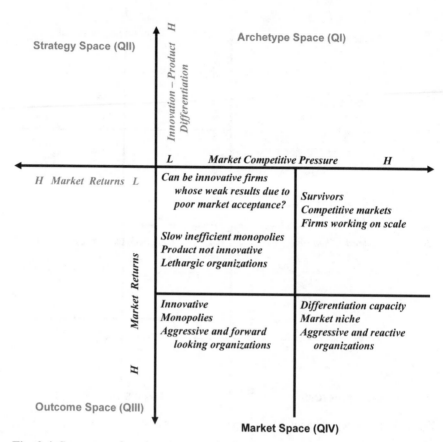

Fig. 3.4. Summary of market structures in the market space

Fig. 3.4 summarises major characteristics of the market space, which locates firms along given competitive market pressure and resulting market share[8].

Notice that in figure, the northwest cell includes innovative firms that have been unable to find market acceptance. Thus the product may have been technologically advanced for instance, but somehow hasn't clicked in the market place. Box 5.2 in Chap. 5 illustrates one such case.

---

[8] This is a summary in that each of the four cells could be subdivided into two sub cells, corresponding to the degree of innovation/product differentiation as being high or low. We avoid this elaboration here in order to focus on the most important aspects of the model.

Box 3.4: The Integrated and the BCG Model

As mentioned earlier, one of the virtues of management models is their simplicity. However there is seldom any theoretical rigor with no behavioural relationship presented in the mostly 2*2 framework of these models. A case in point is the BCG framework.

The BCG model uses two market result variables: *relative market share* and the *growth rates* of the industry. Then, products are ranked in four different categories: cash cows (high market share and low market growth rate), dogs (both low market share and growth rate), question marks (low market share but high market growth) and stars (high market share and growth rate).

We can incorporate the BCG model in the integrated innovation space, as shown in the figure below. The figure illustrates the position of Product, a *star* in the integrated space.

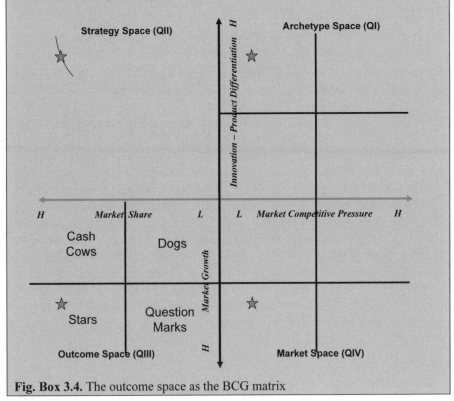

Fig. Box 3.4. The outcome space as the BCG matrix

4 Market Archetypes: the Fox, the Wolf, the Bear and the Sheep

Whatever goes upon two legs is an enemy.
Whatever goes upon four legs, or has wings, is a friend.
No animal shall wear clothes.
No animal shall sleep in a bed with sheets.
No animal shall drink alcohol in excess.
No animal shall kill any other animal without cause.
All animals are equal.

Animal Farm, *George Orwell*

4.1 Introduction

In the previous chapter we presented the analytical framework of the Integrated Model. The three fundamental questions that the model explains are –*where* is a product located in an integrated innovation space, *why* it is so located and which then provides valuable clues to *what* to do when designing strategy.

The Integrated Model describes a product (or single product firm) along four dimensions[1] – an external market dimension, an innovation dimension, and two outcome dimensions. These four dimensions together define four environmental spaces: a product/market space, a strategic environment, an outcome space and a market space. The model unites the four spaces in a single analytical framework creating an integrated innovation space.

In this chapter, we focus on the first quadrant, the archetype space. In this space we describe four major market archetypes characterised by the differences in their competitive market pressure and the degree of product

---

[1] See Box 3.2 in chapter 3 for a definition and explanation of our choice of terminology.

differentiation. Later, in the chapter on the diagnostic framework, we shall explain our choice of metrics which combine different variables to measure competitive pressure and degree of innovation and product differentiation. Sec. 4.3 presents a *radiograph* of the major characteristics of each of the archetypes.

4.2 Archetype Space

Recall that the first quadrant of our model, the archetype space was defined by two dimensions – the degree of competitive market pressure and the degree of innovation-product differentiation. On the horizontal axis, as we move to the right, an industry gets characterised by an increasing number of firms and thus falling under greater competitive pressure. A vertical upward movement in this space on the other hand, reflects an increase in the degree of innovation/product (or brand) differentiation of the firm (product).

Box 4.1: *Innovation* or *Differentiation?*

The integrated innovation space has as its strategic dimension the degree of innovation-differentiation. So, which is when? A literature review (industrial organization, strategy or innovation) doesn't reveal any consistent distinction between these two variables. Indeed the first two strands of literature that we discussed in Chap.2 – industrial organization and management strategy, engage and discuss differentiation.

A reading of these two variables is simple in the integrated model. If a product is in a market characterized by a high degree of competition, and yet is in the upper region of the innovation dimension, then the product is differentiated. However if a product is isolated from competition and being in the upper end of the innovation dimension, then it is innovative product. Thus foxes are differentiated and wolves are innovative!

Differentiation then is given by attributes that distinguish a product from its rivals, which can be pure product attributes or distinct services associated with similar products or vice versa. Innovation is the newness of a product (or service) and can be breakthrough products or superior product performance attributes in relation to close rivals.

We characterize the archetype space into four major product or market archetypes: the *bear*, the *wolf* the *fox* and the *sheep* markets[2] as illustrated in Fig. 4.1 below.

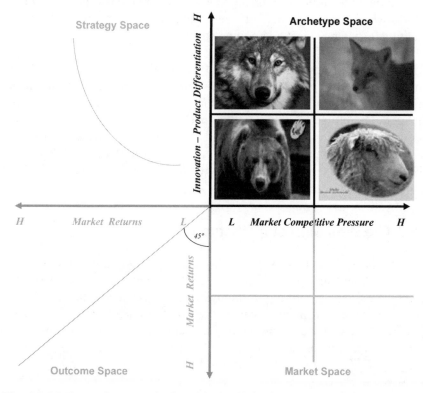

Fig. 4.1. Market archetypes: the *bear,* the *wolf,* the *fox* and the *sheep*

4.2.1 The Bear Market Archetype

This market archetype is characterised by few firms offering products or services that are not very differentiated. The reduced number of firms op-

---

[2] To a certain extent, this is in keeping with the precedence of using metaphors, in business models. The use of metaphors in describing business models however carries certain risks of interpretation. For instance Gunnar Hedlund in his unpublished paper 'Milking Cows vs. Going Hunting: Conceptions of Corporate Strategies' in his criticism of the Boston Consulting Group's use of farm animal metaphors in the BCG model. Cited in http://www.tompeters.com which is Tom Peters blog.

erating in such markets is often due to licensing requirements or the ownership of a scarce resource. The bear market is generally not characterised by free entry and exit. Due to the low degree of competition, market share tends to be high. However this may not translate into correspondingly high profits, which other than market size depend on other factors such as productivity, efficiency, cost and pricing structure.

Many natural monopolies like utility companies are bears, as too are various public enterprises. Firms in bear markets tend to have rigid hierarchical organisations that reflect in their lethargic response to external changes. The protected nature of the market implies that firms characterized as bears tend to be inefficient and also not client oriented. Their survival depends on the extent to which they can protect their market space from encroachment by other potential entrants, and guard zealously their monopoly rights.

4.2.2 The Wolf Market Archetype

Like the bear market the wolf market archetype is characterised by the presence of very few firms offering a similar product or service. However unlike bears, wolves are highly innovative. The reduced number of firms operating in the wolf industry can be the result of one or more factors such as – high entry costs, licensing requirements, patents, technological supremacy, etc. A technologically advanced product such as the *Apple iPod* would be a good example of a wolf product.

Due to their highly innovative and differentiating characteristics, wolves have few direct competitors and consequently enjoy high market shares. This often translates into higher profits but the temporal profit window is determined by the extent to which wolves can be copycatted. This in turn is determined by the sources of innovation of wolf products and the extent to which these sources enjoy some form of sustainability (technological superiority, knowledge, patent ownership etc.).

Product sophistication and not price is the distinguishing characteristic that consumers seek in wolf products. To remain as wolves, these firms have to constantly invest in innovation and in the quality of their human resources. Organizational agility is the key to the sustainability of the innovation strategy. Constantly gazing the horizon for likely competitors and imitators, wolves are aggressive and protect their market share and brand name fiercely. They are also quick to respond and attentive to their client needs and try to maintain client fidelity. Teamwork and creativity are the hallmarks of the wolf organization.

Box 4.2: Identifying the wolves

What are the firms behind wolf products? Indeed if a company continuously churns out wolves, then who are these wolf firms? For one answer, one can turn to the *Wired Magazine* report of its top Wired 40. Although technology biased, the ranking still provides a clue to what makes wolf firms, and of course who are the wolves which have the technological superiority to produce 'killer products'. According to the Wired, the top 40 firms all share strategic vision, global reach and killer technology. These three factors are coupled with what they describe as the 'X-factor' – *"a hunger for new ideas and an impatience to put them into practice."* The following table gives the 2006 Wired 40 ranking.

Table Box 4.2. 2006 Wired Ranking

Rank	Firm	Rank	Firm
1	Google	21	Nvidia
2	Apple	22	Verizon
3	Samsung	23	Flextronics
4	Genentech	24	Intel
5	Yahoo	25	Monsanto
6	Amazon.com	26	EMC
7	Toyota	27	Dupont
8	General Electric	28	Jetblue
9	News Corp.	29	Lenovo
10	SAP	30	TSMC
11	Infosys Tech	31	BP
12	Cisco	32	Li & Fung
13	Electronic Arts	33	Exelon
14	Netflix	34	Costco
15	Salesforce.com	35	Gen-Probe
16	Medtronic	36	Microsoft
17	Sunpower Corp.	37	L-3 Communications
18	IBM	38	Citigroup
19	Ebay	39	Comcast
20	Infospace	40	Pfizer

Source: http://www.wired.com/wired/archive/14.07/wired40.html

Box 4.3: How large are the wolves?

Who tends to be wolves - small or large firms? Early authors including Schumpeter associated innovation with large firms having monopoly power. Market dominance enabled an attitude towards risk taking, necessary for innovation. According to Acs and Audretsch (2003) five factors favour innovation by large firms. The first is the high innovation cost. Second, it was believed that only large firms with market power could appropriate the economic returns of R&D. Third investment in R&D involved taking a risk that larger firms were more capable to bear. Fourth scale economies could generate scope economies in production to R&D. Finally innovation represents in relative terms a major cost to smaller than larger firms.

However empirical studies do not lead to any clear conclusion regarding innovation and firm size. Most studies do confirm that small and medium firms in some sectors contribute to innovation and to technological changes, while in others sectors such as pharmaceutical and biotechnological industries larger firms are associated to innovation. The figure below shows the distribution of R&D expenditure as a percentage of sales, according to firm size in the United States in 2002.

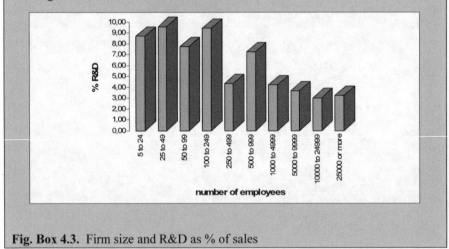

Fig. Box 4.3. Firm size and R&D as % of sales

Many new, breakthrough electronic, telecommunications and sometimes household appliance products with new and superior functionalities can be classified as being in the wolf market as well as software firms. In general technology intensive products, in the *early part of their product life cycles*, can be categorized as wolves.

4.2.3 The Fox Market Archetype

Inhabiting the more competitive market space are firms in the Fox market archetype.

Fox products are highly differentiated as firms try to distinguish themselves in the crowded market space[3]. Firm profits may or may not be significant, depending upon the degree of product differentiation and also on the market size. Foxes face elastic demand curves and they tend to create niche markets. Given the competitive choices available, fox clients are price sensitive so price can be an important strategic variable. Considerable resources can be spent by foxes in advertising in particular and securing client fidelity in general. Product differentiation strategy in such cases is often via marketing, branding differentiation strategies or pricing packages. Firms often bundle their products with services so as to differentiate themselves and not get sucked into the commodity space that is characteristic of sheep market archetypes.

Fox organizations tend to be lean and quick to respond to changing market conditions. Individual creativity finds an important role in the organizational culture.

In the world of business there are numerous examples of firms who could be called foxes in their effort to create market niches through product innovation or brand differentiation. For instance, the computer industry can be considered as an example of the fox market, in their continuous effort to create, for instance in the desktop market, a brand name. The market for clothing, consumer goods, and MBA programs are some examples of fox markets. Various types of consultancy services and in general many specialized service sector SME's can be described as being in the fox market.

4.2.4 The Sheep Market Archetype

The fourth of our market archetypes is the sheep market, characterised by a large number of firms offering a product or service whose characteristics are very similar. At the extreme, this market is characterised by many firms selling a homogenous product, akin to perfectly competitive markets

---

[3] Corresponding to this market archetype would be firms categorised as being monopolistically competitive in economics.

in economics. Firm entry and exit is easy and relatively inexpensive in this market archetype. An individual firm or product in the sheep market, faces an own price elasticity of demand that is relatively high in absolute terms. Sheep products are seen as commodities with very little to differentiate among the choices available in the market, or are at the end of the product life cycle. The key to their survival lies in providing products and services at low prices and catering to large markets.

Just as the firms themselves, sheep market shares tend to be small from these *me too* sheep products. Firms in this highly competitive market tend to be price takers, that is, they have little power to individually determine the price for its homogeneous product offering. Attention to controlling costs is the focus for survival with sporadic attempts at product differentiation through branding and attention to service. Tasks are clearly defined in sheep markets.

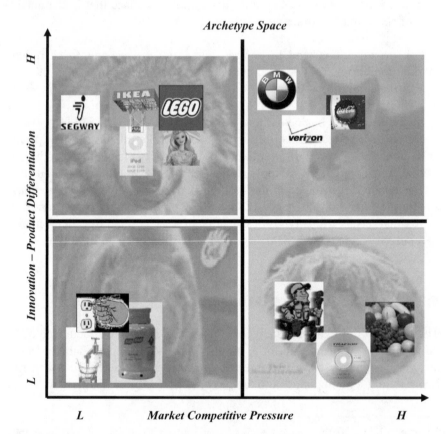

Fig. 4.2. Some products in the archetype space

The agricultural sector can be considered an example of such markets. Small scale construction or specialised service firms like plumbing etc. is another example. Many small and medium enterprises would fall under the sheep market archetype.

Fig. 4.2 suggests (arguably) selected products in each of the four market archetypes. The examples are for illustrative purposes, and only a proper diagnostic using metrics we have developed (see Chap. 10 on the diagnostic framework) can reveal a more elaborate picture.

A summary of some of the major characteristics of firms in each of the four archetypes is given in Fig. 4.3 below.

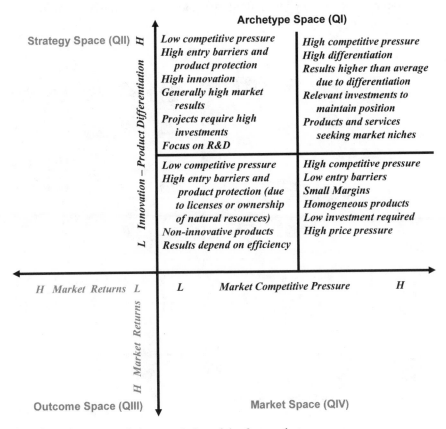

Archetype Space (QI)

Strategy Space (QII)

Innovation – Product Differentiation (H / L)

Low competitive pressure *High entry barriers and product protection* *High innovation* *Generally high market results* *Projects require high investments* *Focus on R&D*	*High competitive pressure* *High differentiation* *Results higher than average due to differentiation* *Relevant investments to maintain position* *Products and services seeking market niches*
Low competitive pressure *High entry barriers and product protection (due to licenses or ownership of natural resources)* *Non-innovative products* *Results depend on efficiency*	*High competitive pressure* *Low entry barriers* *Small Margins* *Homogeneous products* *Low investment required* *High price pressure*

H Market Returns L   L   *Market Competitive Pressure*   H

H Market Returns

Outcome Space (QIII)   Market Space (QIV)

Fig. 4.3. Some general characteristics of the four archetypes

4.3 A Radiograph of Market Archetypes

Market archetypes of the bear, wolf, fox and sheep have some distinguishing characteristics that enable us to perform diagnostics. In Chap. 10, we explain the *diagnostic framework* which permits analyses of firms, positioning them in the integrated framework along the three dimensions of the model: external environment, strategic orientation and outcome(s). The diagnostics also enable detection of *gaps* between firm position and their markets and market leaders as well as intra-firm *gaps*. This latter gap analyses could be for instance, the difference between product differentiation and client's perception of this differentiation. For instance, a firm may consider its product to be distinct from its rivals, but consumers could perceive the product to be very similar. Furthermore organizational mismatch – the gap between organizational culture and firm and market position can also be analyzed[4].

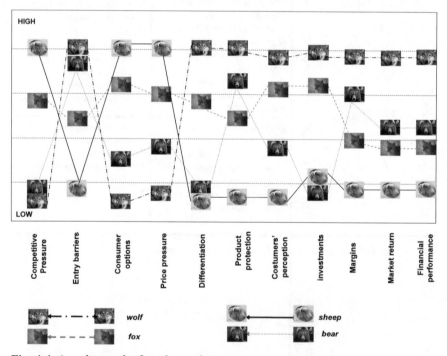

Fig. 4.4. A *radiograph* of market archetypes

---

[4] Chapter 11 relates some organizational issues, although not in a systematic manner. Analyses and diagnostics of the gap or mismatch between organizational culture and product archetype are left as a future endeavour.

Although Chap. 10 explores the diagnostic matrix in detail, Fig. 4.4 above illustrates major characteristics in each market archetype described in our model in the previous section. The eleven characteristics of this figure are related are based on the diagnostic tool we have developed to position a product in the integrated innovation space (and not just archetype space) and market outcome(s). Each one of these characteristics is in turn described by a set of variables.

The eleven characteristics used to plot a product's radiograph in the archetype space are the following:

- Competitive pressure
- Entry barriers
- Consumer options
- Price pressure
- Differentiation
- Product protection
- Consumers' protection
- Investments
- Margins
- Market return
- Financial performance

Note that the *radiograph* doesn't represent any actual example but indicative of the median characteristics of market archetypes – the bear, the wolf, the fox and the sheep, that were presented in Sect. 4.2 earlier. The radiograph is merely indicative of median characteristics of market archetypes – the bear, the wolf, the fox and the sheep.

Fig 4.5 illustrates the radiograph of two major international brands: Ikea and Benetton. The radiographic is suggestive of the relative position along each of the 11 characteristics used.

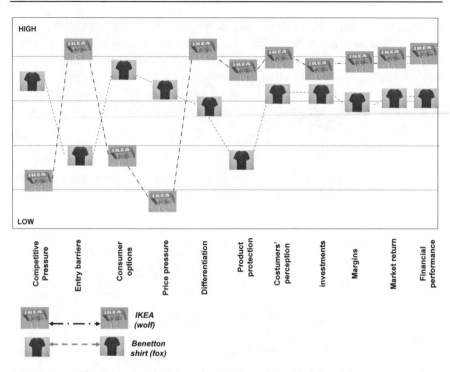

Fig. 4.5. An illustrative *radiograph* for IKEA and Benetton

Box 4.4: Where are the entrepreneurs?

Recall from our discussion earlier in chap. 1 on some definitions of innovation. While Schumpeter's definition finds prominent place in innovation studies, no less important is his definition of an entrepreneur. According to Schumpeter (1934):

"The entrepreneur is the innovator who implements change within markets through the carrying out of new combinations. These new combinations can take several forms;
1) the introduction of a new good or quality thereof,
2) the introduction of a new method of production,
3) the opening of a new market,
4) the conquest of a new source of supply of new materials or parts,
5) the carrying out of the new organization of any industry."

(continued)

Box 4.4: Where are the entrepreneurs? (cont.)

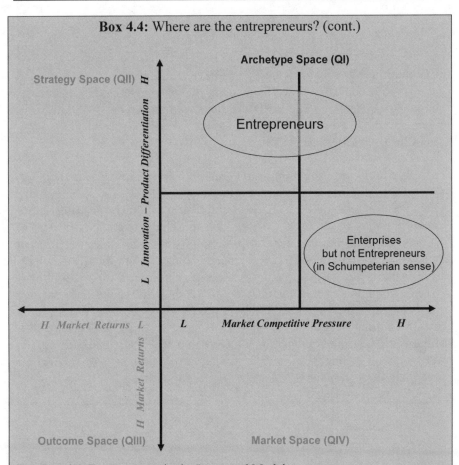

Fig. Box 4.4. Entrepreneurs in the Integrated Model

In the archetype space, which is the entrepreneur's territory? If someone sets up another neighbourhood café, is he an entrepreneur? An entrepreneur, in the Schumpeterian sense is the creator of the 'new' or substantial improvements of the existing, would be hungrily stalking wolf territory. Some may even be in the fox territory as they fight to distinguish themselves from the pack. A good example is Britain's Richard Branson whose diverse products all face strong competition, yet Virgin manages or strives to constantly offer differentiated products, achieving this sometimes via bundling with services or vice versa.

(continued)

Box 4.4: Where are the entrepreneurs? (cont.)

Gartner (1989) considers entrepreneurs as those who create new organizations, who could be either innovators or non innovators. In that sense, some entrepreneurs could also fall in the sheep archetype, as the previous figure shows. According to Gartner, entrepreneurship ends when the process of firm's creation is concluded.

Interestingly the annual report on country comparisons of entrepreneurship produced jointly by Babson College and London Business School, the Global Entrepreneurship Monitor (Minniti et al., 2006), measures entrepreneurial activity closer to Gartner than to Schumpeter. The 2005 GEM report measures entrepreneurship in a country by accounting for nascent entrepreneurs and new business owners. The former are those "who have taken some action toward creating a new business in the past year", between 18 and 64 years. They have to "own a share of the business they are starting and the business must not have paid any wages or salaries for more than three months". On the other hand, "owner-manager of firms are classified as new business owners if the entrepreneurs report that they are active as owner-managers of new firms that have paid wages or salaries for more than three months, but less than 42 months."

5 Metamorphoses: Market Archetypes, Innovation and Integrated Dynamics

Full sail, I voyage
Over the boundless ocean, and I tell you
Nothing is permanent in all the world.
All things are fluent; every image forms,
Wondering through change. Time is itself a river
In constant movement...
That which has been, is not; and that which was not,
Begins to be.

Metamorphoses, *Ovid*

5.1 Metamorphoses

Approximately 2000 years ago, the Roman poet Ovid wrote a classic poem called *The Metamorphoses*. The 15 books in the poem describe the creation and history of the world in terms of Roman and Greek mythology, where constant transformation of the gods takes place. Today products, activities, firms and indeed whole economies are increasingly witnessing another type of metamorphosis as both product life cycles and geography get compressed.

While innovation remains the key to growth, innovative firms are being constantly upstaged by start-ups. Product managers watch with dismay as their most innovative products, fruit of years of research, design, planning and investment, hurtle their way into commoditization. And competition is not just from the ones you knew. Global challengers are coming up everywhere, and now increasingly from developing economies.

The integrated framework presented in Cap. 3 permits an understanding of many of these changes. To design strategy consistent with desired aims requires an understanding of market dynamics. The Integrated Model equips us with tools not just to understand the *where* and the *why* (of a firm's location in the innovation market space), but also the `what´ happens in market dynamics. Equipped with knowledge gained from an integrated analyses one can then design and implement meaningful strategy, the 'what' (to do).

Firms in the different market archetypes described in the previous chapter metamorphose due to a wide variety of forces, both due to changes in the internal and the external market environment. Our model can explain how these forces lead firms to evolve over time, and also help firms design strategies to predict and to emerge on top of these forces. Built around three integrated dimensions – an external environment (market pressure), strategic orientation (innovation-product differentiation) and market results or outcome (sales, market share or profits), the model provides an analytical set of tools that is capable of explaining and even predicting much of the real world firm and market behaviour in one unifying framework.

The protected bear in a market characterised today by a few firms and low degree of differentiation, could suddenly find itself surrounded by foxes and has to learn to adapt rapidly and grow. It has to learn to live with the foxes, populating a market space with a larger number of firms furiously trying to fend off competitors and desperately trying to create market niches. The lone wolf, highly innovative and highly profitable could wake up to see an upstart new born with a new business model that suddenly threatens his market leadership. A few missteps could turn this wolf into irrelevance.

In this chapter we explore some of these dynamics of innovation using the integrated framework. This chapter provides us with the theoretical analytical tools that would help us understand actual market *innovation turbulence*. In Chaps. 6 through 8 we shall use the integrated framework to illustrate various cases and the analyses of dynamics in this chapter is useful for case studies.

The following sections illustrate some key market dynamics using the analytical framework of the Integrated Model. Some of the issues we shall explore include an understanding of the product life cycle, of the process whereby firms try to maintain their market position, of innovation for growth and other related dynamics (see Box 5.1 below). The Integrated Model can be a powerful framework of real world analyses, not just for academics but for practitioners and management. Not all dynamics are explained here, and we leave it to the reader to explore further dynamic applications based on the Integrated Model.

Box 5.1: Integrated dynamics

The Integrated Model permits analyses of some of the diverse dynamics that play out in the market place. The analytical framework used in this chapter to illustrate some of the market dynamics. Later chapters would illustrate some actual case studies using the integrated framework.

Some of the dynamics that we explore using the analytical matrix include:
- Impact of increased competition.
- Explaining product life cycle and different dynamics of (ever shortening product life cycle)
- Innovation (incremental) struggle for mantaining market position
- Explores some dynamics of disruptive innovation
- Explains different Why´s! For instance:
    - Why do two firms which face similar market pressure yet have very different market outcomes
    - How can one explain that two firms can have similar market share but different profit margins
- Explores the issue of sustainability of innovation

It should be reiterated that the analytical framework is open to a vast array of applications, some beyond the scope of this book, and others which we hope to pursue in future work or other researchers may wish to pursue.

5.2 Integrated Dynamics: An Increase in Market Competition

Let us start with the study of an innovative product, a wolf enjoying considerable market domination, high margins and high profits. Her position is shown as **1** in Fig. 5.1 below (where in the outcome space the variable is taken to be a general measure of market outcome for simplicity). However as new products appear in the horizon, with similar characteristics and price competitiveness, her market dominance gets progressively threatened. The increased competition causes the wolf to move increasingly to the right in the archetype space, with a corresponding inward shift of the IP curve in the second quadrant.

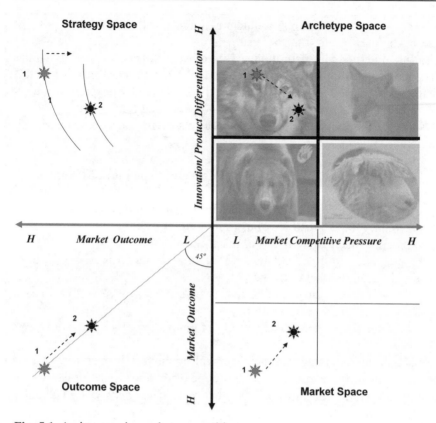

Fig. 5.1. An increase in market competition

With more competitors, the 'newness' of the product gets diminished. The wolf finds itself in a new position (**2** in Fig. 5.1) that leaves her with a diminished market outcome (market share, margins or profits). This dynamic traces itself out in the integrated innovation space as we can see in from Fig. 5.1. In the fourth quadrant (the market space), increased competition is reflected in the diminished market outcome from position as illustrated in Fig 5.1.

5.3 Integrated Dynamics: Explaining Product Life Cycle

Factors such as increased global competition, fast evolution of information technology and an increasingly demanding and price sensitive clientele with more control over the purchase process, via the built to order (BTO) business model for instance, are all contributing to the shrinking life cycle of a product. Fig. 5.2a below illustrates how short product life cycles are fast becoming. As the figure illustrates, the entire product life cycle is increasingly getting squeezed into the time that it once took just to get the product into the market.

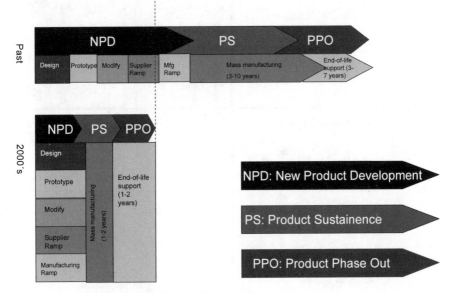

Fig. 5.2a. Shrinking product life cycle

We can further take our analyses of the previous section (dynamics of increased competition) to explain the product life cycle. As the competition heats up, the wolf can fast find itself metamorphosed into a sheep. This describes a product life cycle whereby increased competition takes a firm (product) from a wolf to a fox to sheep, where it can end up becoming a *commodity*. The corresponding positions are illustrated in Fig. 5.2b below, where the wolf (**1**) metamorphosizes into the fox (**2**) and then into the sheep (**3**). Note that in the strategy space the IP curve shifts inward, implying that with an increase in competitive pressure, the market returns decrease for a given degree of product differentiation.

The shrinking life span of a product with the impending prospect of commoditization and accelerated obsolescence of even very innovative products is explored at some depth in Chap. 8. In that chapter we discuss the omnipresent threat of commoditization.

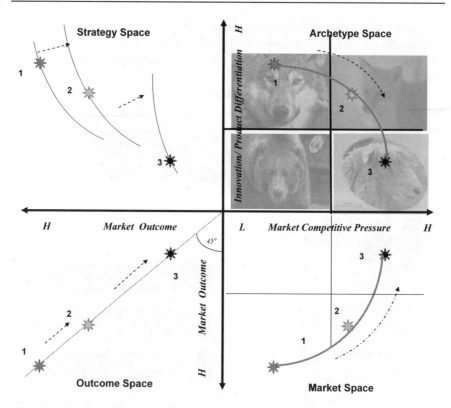

Fig. 5.2b. Product life cycle in the Integrated Model

The situation described in Fig. 5.2b is the process of decreased market returns from an increase in competition, assuming that a firm doesn't make efforts (or has no capacity for) to innovate/differentiate its product. However, a firm could and should fight back, a case that is described in the following section (see also Chap. 8).

Box 5.2: Innovation and outcome

That the emphasis of market result is one fundamental analysis permitted by the integrated innovation model, is by now familiar. This preoccupation with outcome of innovation is evident in that outcome variables are built explicitly in the model. We can think of very innovative products (the *Segway Human Transporter* comes to mind), which has not met with the desired outcome in the market place.

(continued)

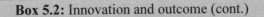

Box 5.2: Innovation and outcome (cont.)

In the strategy space therefore (and consequently reflected in the outcome and market spaces) the outcome (measured in any way) is much less than desired or expected. The figure below illustrates a case of the failure of innovation in terms of expected results. Segway is an innovative product but whose market results have so far been disappointing.

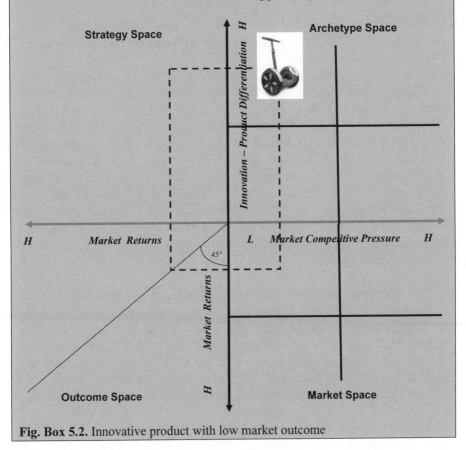

Fig. Box 5.2. Innovative product with low market outcome

5.4 Competition and Innovation Dynamics: Alice in Innovation Land

Let us revisit our wolf. Highly innovative, as a result of investment of enormous resources, enjoying significant margins and associated profits, this wolf is suddenly attacked by another firm, whose product threatens the wolf's grip on the market. The wolf slips. Her market share reduces as do her profits. But the wolf is determined to strike back. It knows that attack is the best form of defence and of recovery of market share. And attack she does. By innovating and trying to move up its innovation payoff curve (IP). While she is not able to recover her earlier market position completely, she is nevertheless able to regain most of it.

And this story is repeated over and over again. Not just by many firms, but by the same firm many times. Always on the innovation path, which is the only way to stay ahead.

The Integrated Model is a very useful analytical tool to explain how this market place dynamic works. In Fig. 5.3 below, the wolf is located in position **1** in the archetype space (and tracing out her corresponding locations in the integrated space), which shows its competitive position and associated market outcome. With the arrival of new rivals, the degree of market pressure increases, causing her position to shift in the archetype space from position **1** to **2**. The corresponding dislocations are shown in the other three quadrants. However with greater competition, the product has also lost some of its lustre. It is no longer as innovative as before, and in a sense she has slipped ground on the innovation curve as well, to position **3** as illustrated in Fig. 5.3.

With the threat of an even greater market share loss looming, the wolf has to invest and focus on innovation. There is no other way to regaining its competitiveness and growth. This it does by moving up its IP curve (shown by the curve in red in strategy space) to a new (temporary) position **4**. This innovation strategy pays off in the form of recovering some lost ground, as the figure illustrates. The inlay box in the strategy space gives a magnified view of the innovation fight back. And this process continues.

The only way to break out of this cycle is if the wolf manages to come up with a radically new product, which will enable her to once again be the master of the innovation landscape. Till the cycle plays itself out again. And just like in Alice's wonderland, it takes all the running to keep in the same place. If not, the firm may very soon find itself on the path to commoditization.

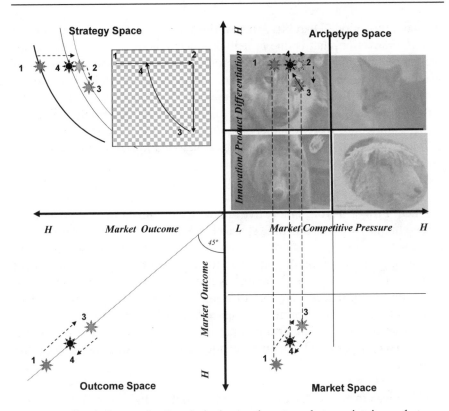

Fig. 5.3. Alice in Innovation Land: the innovation struggle to maintain market position

5.5 Disruptive Innovation

In Chap. 2 where we did a quick tour of some important strands in innovation literature, we presented the process of disruptive innovation as studied by Clayton Christensen[1]. The fundamental question asked was why even some of the best run firms lose their leadership position? Christensen researched on whether a given innovation is sustaining or disruptive to the established companies in a given industry. As mentioned in Chap. 2, by sustaining innovations, Christensen referred to innovations that contribute to improved performance in existing products and thereby a strengthening of each respective company's position on the market, similar to incre-

---

[1] See Christensen (1997).

mental innovation. Disruptive innovations on the other hand is almost *stealth* innovation, that is due to new products that at least on some attributes are worse than in the existing product, but can lead to the failure of leading companies in the industry. In sustaining circumstances, he found that incumbent firms almost always prevail. However there could also be circumstances where the challenge is to produce a simpler product either to new customers or to less demanding customers. Christensen and Raynor[2] defined these two types of disruption as new-market disruption and low-end disruption respectively.

The Integrated Model illustrates the case of *low end disruption*. The incumbent firm, is a wolf, innovative and with a dominant market position as represented by **I** in the outcome space (Fig.5.4). It has pursued a sustaining innovation strategy, the innovation payoff curve **I'-I'** to the left marking its passage as it continually improved its product offering. The incumbent wolf caters to a consumer base that is at the upper end of the preference spectrum, given that the product offering is innovative and sophisticated. This leaves a consumer preference space that still has many less demanding and even possibly hitherto non participating consumers (new market). Vector **I-III** gives an idea of the magnitude of the market *ignored* by the incumbent.

Consider now the entry of a low end disruptor (and eventually a hybrid disruptor). In the outcome space this *birth* of the firm is shown by the emergence of a new firm **O** in the Fig 5.4. The entrant offering is a simpler and less expensive product that appeals to less demanding customers. Having gained a foothold in the market, the disruptor enters into its own sustainable innovation path and moves up from **1** to **2** as shown in the IP curve of the disruptor. Till this point the incumbent has not considered the entrant a threat, indeed because the market the entrant served was at the low end with both prices and margins being low. This enabled the incumbent to focus on its more demanding customers, as explained by Christensen in his model.

However the sustaining innovation path pursued by the entrant suddenly brings it in the radar of the wolf incumbent, once it attracts clients from the incumbent firm. But by then it is too late. Both, market share captured and the product sophistication of the entrant is enough to cause a significant erosion of market share, as we can see in the inward shift of the IP from **I** to **II** in the outcome space.

---

[2] See Christensen and Raynor (2003).

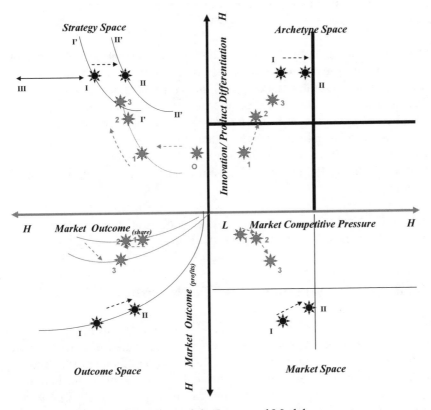

Fig. 5.4. Disruptive innovation and the Integrated Model

The integrated framework enables us to understand the disruption phenomenon in a very satisfying manner. The outcome space has two variables, market share and profit margins. Their relationship is shown by the concave market return curve. For the wolf, till the disruption took place, she enjoyed a high market share and high profits as shown in the Fig. 5.4. Firm position **I**, traces out the entire story of the incumbent, from archetype space to the business space, where the latter illustrates the market competition – margin situation. Disruption brings about decreased market share, decreased margins and thrusts the wolf in a more dangerous competitive environment, as illustrated by situation **II** of the wolf.

For the disruptor, the story is the reverse. Having eaten into the market share of the wolf, the entrant increasingly improves its market position. However as depicted in this particular illustration, sustaining innovation leading to increased market share, still doesn't translate into greatly increased profits (movement of the entrant from **1** to **2** in the outcome space).

However, the disruptor is able not only to eat into the market share of the wolf by its increasingly sophisticated offering, but is also able to attract people hitherto not in the marketplace (*non consumers* according to Christensen and Raynor). One way we can illustrate this new market disruption phenomenon, is via the shift downward of the market share-margin curve. The disruptor then enjoys a much higher profit margin and position **3** in the figure illustrates this process. An (upward) shift of the incumbent's curve in quadrant III (not shown) would reflect its increasingly cornered position.

The entrant could eventually becoming a wolf (not shown) and the erstwhile wolf moving closer to fox territory or into oblivion.

5.6 Integrated Dynamics: And Tell Me Why...

The Integrated Model permits analyses of a wide range of market dynamics besides the previous four cases illustrated. Indeed, as we shall see later, much of real world dynamics is often a combination of some of the movements explained. Looking back at some industrial organization literature, some of the analytics studied in therein can perhaps far more simply, explained using the visual framework of the model.

Let us take the case of one such question: how can we explain two firms facing a similar degree of market pressure, but whose outcomes (in terms of market shares, margins or profits)? The integrated framework illustrates this case in a simple and visually appealing manner.

In Fig. 5.5, two foxes **1** and **2**, inhabit the same market space populated by many firms. The market pressure on both is therefore similar. The more wily and resourceful fox, however has made every effort to differentiate herself to make herself more distinguishable in this crowded market as we can see in the figure where firm (product) **1** is located higher up in the fox archetype space than **2**. (This may imply that **1** is situated further to the left in the archetype space than **2**, but for sake of simplicity we ignore this detail). The outcome space in this illustration, distinguishes between two types of market outcomes- market share and profits. Their relationship is plotted by the concave outcome curve in the outcome space[3]. Assuming that the margins are similar, this would still lead to **1** receiving a payoff from its differentiation effort. This can be seen by the higher profits of the differentiating fox **1**, which is seen in the market space in Fig.5.5.

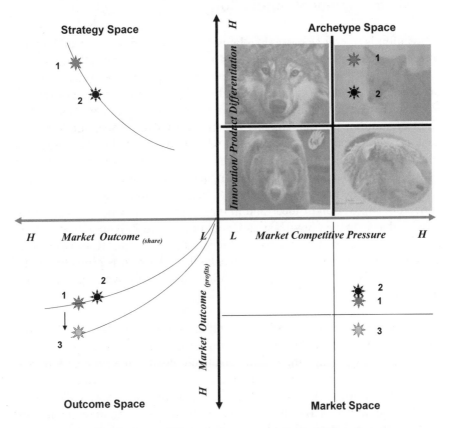

Fig. 5.5. An illustration of a differentiation strategy in similar market space

Now if the margins[4] of the first fox were also higher, then we can see this reflected in the more downward outcome curve in the third quadrant as

---

[3] As in the previous case of disruptive innovation, it is illustrative to distinguish between two types of market outcomes. The generic convex curve reflects diminishing returns (profits) from increased market share.

[4] This could be the result of a combination of variety of forces - aggressive cost cutting, a more profitable market niche due to its higher product differentiation, greater productivity etc. This analyses presented here assumes that greater differentiation has not led to significant changes in market size of each, that is to say, both firms are selling to the same consumer space.

shown in Fig. 5.5. This would then lead to an even higher profit payoff for the differentiating fox, as indicated by position **3** in the third quadrant.

5.7 Sustainability of Innovation

Innovation is of course more than launching new products. A search on the internet reveals myriad interpretations and usage of the word "innovation." Besides a new product or service, new ideas and new business strategies and business models (the Dell model for instance) are also innovations. With so many interpretations of the word *innovation* it is very easy to lose sight of some of the fundamental questions involved when studying newness or innovation. First is of course why innovate? As we have seen the Integrated Model explicitly introduces outcome variables in the strategy and outcome spaces to analyze the impact of innovation and product differentiation. The second question that comes to mind, especially in the context of innovation of ideas and in many services, is what protects 'newness'? That is to say, how easy is it for someone to imitate a new idea for instance? While in the case of products, patents, technical knowledge or cutting edge technology applications can all work towards protecting innovation, at least for some time, this is often not the case with ideas or many services.

A new idea, which can be novel and effective in its desired objective, can quickly be copied. Two possibilities arise. First, the idea can be a one shot idea (with perhaps the originator of the idea having no desire to pursue it repeatedly. This can be termed as a 'one shot innovation game'). Pursuit of the idea either by the originator or imitators may result in the outcome being very different from that of the original. An outcome may be positive the first round only and thereafter both the originator and imitators find that repeated implementation draws unfavourable outcomes.

The second possibility can be that the new idea or service is truly effective, bringing about the desired outcome, with imitators too realizing positive outcomes. However the idea no longer remains an *innovation* in that once copied it is no longer new, but none the less remains effective and becomes the best practice for the industry.

Box 5.3: Why is innovation is linked to technology?

The literature on innovation is replete with references to, and indeed often based on technology. This is given the general consensus that technology is the driver of innovation.

Possession of superior technology affords protection of innovation that provides some degree of sustainability. Which is one reason why innovation that is not technology based (i.e. not amenable to some protection) as in most activities in the service sector, has a small window of opportunity to leverage innovation. This also implies that there innovation investments in the form of R&D are high. Protection need not be just in the form of patents but also certain types of special knowledge. Protection helps to provide some 'stickiness' in the markets.

Comparing price-to-earnings (P/E) ratio as well as their growth and earnings per share, between technology companies and financial companies indicate that values for the former are generally higher with much more growth potential.

The following table is an illustration of returns linked to core technology companies (as well as firms such as Toyota which has a long history of innovation), which compares P/E ratios of some technology to non technology firms.

Table Box 5.3. P/E ratios of technology and non technology firms (Dec, 2006)

Firm	P/E ratio
Google	61,7
InfoSys	45,7
Apple	40,1
Microsoft	23,3
Walt Disney	20,4
Toyota	14,7
Goldman Sachs	12,2
Nissan	10,5
ABN Amro holdings	10,0

(continued)

Box 5.3: Why innovation is linked to technology? (cont.)

In a survey conducted by IBM's Global Business Service, 765 CEOs, business executives and public sector leaders from around the world, senior management viewed enormous benefits through the integration of business and technology. Fig. Box 5.3 illustrates the benefits from such an integration, results from IBM's survey (see also Sect. 11.1 of Chap. 11).

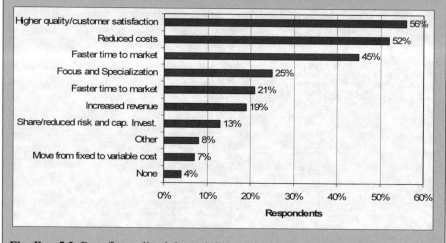

Fig. Box 5.3. Benefits realized through integration of business and technology

Source: The Global CEO Survey 2006

The internet has become fertile ground for breeding many new ideas with the word 'innovation' tacked to these ideas. One such can be found in a recent story that caught one's imagination. A Canadian man started with a large red paper clip and a dream – to trade it up via the Internet. Trade up till he could end up with a house. And he did! In fourteen trades, he was able to get a house[5] in July 2006, one year after he started on this journey. It is illustrative to use the Integrated Model to analyze whether this sort of 'innovation' of ideas, and indeed for much of the service sector.

The other interesting case of sustainability (or stickiness) of ideas is illustrated in Figs. 5.6.a. and 5.6.b. In the first case, we take the example of the idea of trading of the paper clip.

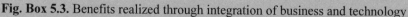

[5] One can see the picture of the house and all the trades he did on the site http://oneredpaperclip.blogspot.com/

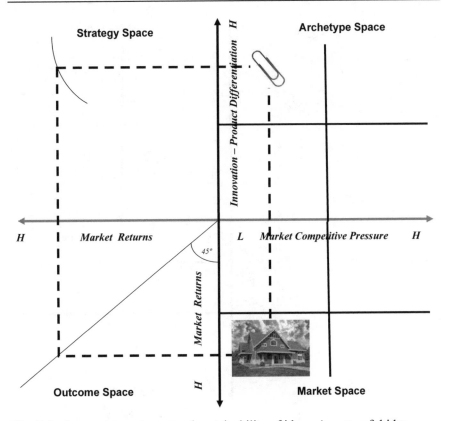

Fig. 5.6a. Innovation: outcome and sustainability of ideas. A successful idea

After the initial success, if an imitator was to imitate the idea or try to implement some variant of this idea, it is unlikely to result in something anywhere close to the original outcome. Let's take the example of another cybernaut, fascinated by the success of the paper clip trade, and decides to embark on another trading voyage, this time a pencil. The novelty of the original idea being lost, it quickly wears off with imitation, with the new trade offering fundamentally little of intrinsic value to the market place. Fig. 5.6.b. illustrates a possible hypothetical outcome of such a trade!

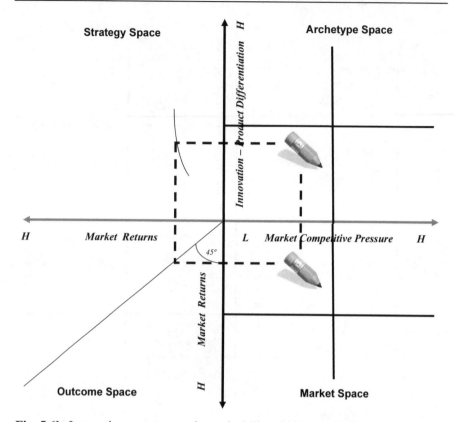

Fig. 5.6b. Innovation: outcome and sustainability of ideas. Imitating an idea.

A repeat of such an idea such as this is fraught with the danger of both losing the innovativeness as well as the impact of the repeat. The fictional repeat, a yellow clip is a sheep, with no return!

5.8 Innovation Through M&A?

In an effort to maintain leadership position, companies who can't innovate or unable to deliver innovation results with current efforts often look at outside sources to give it the innovation edge. This innovation edge can be *acquired* by trying to buying innovation off the shelf through mergers and acquisitions (M&A). Writing in Strategy & Leadership, researchers Muller, Välikangas and Merlyn make this point forcefully[6]:

---

[6] See Muller et al. (2005).

"In an effort to maintain a leadership position, companies that can't innovate must buy innovation off the shelf. For example, as the fizz went out of the carbonated drinks market in recent years, Coca-Cola acquired Mad River Traders and PepsiCo bought South Beach Beverage Company— both makers of alternative beverages such as bottled waters, juices, and teas laced with ginseng. Though sometimes effective in the short term, this strategy of innovation through acquisition usually fails because the acquiring corporation overestimates the value of synergies and underestimates the post-merger integration difficulties. In any case, innovation by acquisition is always at enormous cost, either in cash or stock, to the shareholders of the acquiring corporation. Shareholders see far higher returns when companies successfully innovate organically."

Many of the mergers and acquisitions motivated by the desire to acquire a competitive edge fail to create the promised growth. Some statistics show that the failure rate of most mergers and acquisitions lies somewhere between 40-80%, with roots not owing to financial, monetary and legal issues but to corporate cultural differences

Using the example of M&A in the auto industry, Gary Hamel, terms the M&A trend as the mating of dinosaurs, concluding that "You don't get a gazelle by breeding dinosaurs."[7]

The M&A trend is not confined to traditional companies, and is catching up in the internet sphere as well. In search of new high growth markets old media companies are in the hunt of successful online companies, such as News Corporation buying the social networking site MySpace and NBC aquiring iVillage. Pure internet players are also in the hunt, witness Yahoo's acquisition of photo sharing site Flickr or eBay's buying up Skype and Google acquiring YouTube.

An M&A dynamic is illustrated in Fig. 5.7 below. Two firms **1** and **2** holding respective market shares of 45% and 20%. Firm **1** is the older firm with the dominant market share as compared to the newer firm **2**. However, **2** is the more innovative new firm, and despite its lower market share, enjoys higher profits than **1**. The acquisition of **2** by **1**, in the hope of *buying innovation* may not work, a case that we illustrate in this example (Fig. 5.7). The mating of the fox with the wolf in this illustration has resulted in worse results for both and decrease in share holder value. The downward shift of the curve relating market share to profits (outcome

---

[7] The Wall Street Journal Online, 22nd January, available at http://www.strategos. com/articles/dinosaurs.htm

space) from X_1 and X_2 to Y as shown in the figure is due to the mismatch and post merger troubles belying market expectations.

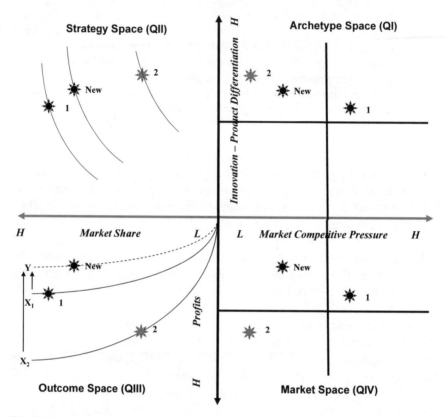

Fig. 5.7. M&A and the Integrated Model

6 Sustaining Innovation: Staying Ahead

> Now here, you see, it takes all the running you can do,
> to keep in the same place. If you want to get somewhere else,
> you must run at least twice as fast as that!
>
> Alice in Wonderland, *Lewis Carroll*

6.1 Sustaining Innovation

For an innovator to stay ahead, the road is fraught with constant challenges. Nothing typifies modern capitalism more than the constant churn that takes place at the top, in today's market place. Schumpeter illustrated this process in his famous observation on the *creative destruction* that takes place in modern economies. As he observed in 1942[1].

> "The opening up of new markets and the organizational development from the craft shop and factory to such concerns as US Steel illustrate the process of industrial mutation that incessantly revolutionizes the economic structure from within, incessantly destroying the old one, incessantly creating a new one ... [The process] must be seen in its role in the perennial gale of creative destruction; it cannot be understood on the hypothesis that there is a perennial lull."

Firms and products once considered exemplars of innovation, find their status extremely short-lived. For instance, in their classic in 1982, Tom Peters and Robert Waterman[2] cited Atari, Wang, Amdahl, Texas Instruments, Eastman Kodak, and Maytag as excellent companies. Some of these firms are nowhere to be found today or are far from being shining stars of innovation[3]. Twelve years later, James Collins and Jerry Porras[4] looked at 18

---

[1] See Schumpeter (1942).

[2] See Peters and Waterman (1982).

[3] A 2002 article in Forbes magazine however found that contrary to popular notion, many of the companies identified by the authors as excellent actually

well known, established and healthy companies (*visionaries*). Now many of these visionaries are hard to find. Today's innovators include a crop of firms like Apple, Amazon, Wal-Mart, Southwest Airlines, eBay, Dell, Google are all relative newcomers. Ten years from now, perhaps we would most likely be speaking of other new stars: Skype, Virgin or Infosys, among others.

The volatility at the innovator's table suggests that the real issue today is not just how to innovate, but also how to sustain this innovation? The window of opportunity opened up by an innovation is remarkably short, and sooner or later the innovation crown goes to the challenger that comes up with an even better product. In Chaps. 7 and 8 we study different cases-Lego, Barbie, Netscape and Internet Explorer, Google and Yahoo, innovators all and the slippery slope that they all face. Those chapters analyze these firms in the context of the struggle to maintain leadership and in some cases the impending threat of commoditization that they face.

In this chapter however, we use a case study to understand the dynamics of sustaining leadership, not in the context of ideas (as discussed in sec. 5.7 in the previous chapter) but of products. We review the case of the iconic Apple iPod, whose biggest challenger is as yet not imminent, but who however is constantly churning up updates of its MP3 player. The story related here is not so much a struggle but of how innovation stars are no longer content with just being at the top, but trying to make sure that any incumbent to its throne has a hard task catching up.

6.2 Apple iPod: Staying Ahead

Thirty years ago, *apple* was a fruit. Today when one *googles*[5] the word the primary references to *apple* are no longer associated with the fruit[6], but to the Silicon Valley technology firm Apple Inc. The firm is the maker of two of the most innovative products today, the Macintosh personal computer

---

turned out to be star performers in the twenty year period since the list came out!

[4] See Collins and Porras (1994).

[5] A term which has become a verb has now entered the Merriam Webster dictionary signifying using the Google search engine to look for information on the World Wide Web.

[6] In a recent search, the first thirty five search results all were with respect to the consumer electronics giant!

and the portable MP3 player, the iPod. After a rocky period Apple is now a celebrated innovator, the toast of Wall Street. Not just because of its superbly designed Apple *Powerbook*, but more recently because of its Apple iPod (and the iPod mini) which since its introduction in the market in October of 2001, has sold approximately sixty million units!

The history of the iPod is an excellent illustration of how successful products constantly innovate despite the absence of a clear imminent threat. The very first version of the iPod which was released in October of 2001[7] had a disk capacity of 5gigabytes (GB) with a capability to hold 1000 songs. Small, sleek and superbly designed, it was priced at $399. At that time, few industry watchers were willing to bet on the product. It was expensive and the technology already existed[8]. A portable MP3 player was also not new, there were other hard drive based music players in the market at that time[9]. But the iPod's small hard disk made the player much smaller than the rivals, and its intuitive design made the iPod attractive to its customers. What was most outstanding was that it offered a *music listening experience*. The iPod had a set of tiny, glistening white, distinctive earbud headphones.

Almost ten months earlier in the same year (10th January, 2001), Apple had created iTunes, a program that converted audio CDs into compressed digital audio files, organized digital music collections, and played Internet radio[10]. The iPod used a high speed *FireWire* interface to transfer files on and off of it from the iTunes web site, which was a true innovation. Despite the doubts of many, this pairing of iPod to iTunes proved to be a hit, with the iPod selling 125000 units by the end of 2001.

---

[7] Amidst great secrecy, the first iPod was unveiled in a ceremony on October 23, 2001, trumpeted as "Not Macintosh".

[8] The German research institute Fraunhofer IIS developed the original MP3 codec, and co developed (with Sony, AT&T and others) the AAC format used by Apple in the iPod. See also Box 6.1.

[9] To know a little of the history of mp3 visit the site (one among others) http://inventors.about.com/od/mstartinventions/a/MPThree.htm

[10] Once again there were other companies who did all these at that time, notably the firm Napster which allowed free music downloads from its site.

Since 2001, there have so far been five generations[11] of the iPod, the latest, the iPod 5 was released in 12th October 2005[12]. While maintaining its appealing design, each generation of the iPod came with ever more hard disk space (capable of storing more number of songs). Although the price has generally varied between $300 to $500 (depending about the hard disk space), the price per gigabyte has constantly been coming down (see Fig 6.1).

Every generation of the iPod has represented an improvement over the previous generation which its competitors have not been able to match so far, although there are quite a few that are nipping the heels (including Microsoft's *Zune* MP3 player). Table 6.1 illustrates the major features and incremental innovations of each successive incarnation starting from the second[13]. It must be said that to the non music buff (to which the author pleads guilty) all five generations were roughly similar in appearance, weight and features. Each generation, incrementally improved upon the earlier generation.

One of the major incremental innovations that the second generation represented over the first was the replacement of the original mechanical scroll wheel with a sensitive non mechanical one, which was called the *touch wheel*. Other improvements were in hard disks that were bigger but marginally heavier and compatibility with the windows operating system[14]. The prices of the iPods (for the same sizes as the original generation) were lowered as we can see from Table 6.2 and Fig 6.1.

---

[11] Despite these five generations, iPod has other versions, like the iPod mini, iPod nano and iPod shuffle and also other special editions, like versions signed by Madonna or U2, an iPod Nike or an iPod Harry Potter and even an iPod nano Red promoted by Oprah and Bono!

[12] Almost to the date that iPod celebrates 5 years, n the 23rd of October.

[13] For research and material used in this chapter, besides the official iPod web site (www.apple.com/ipod) and Wikipedia, other sites that were also consulted, including   http://www.ilounge.com/index.php/articles/comments/instant-expert-a-brief-history-of-ipod/ and http://www.applematters.com/.

[14] For music buffs and technology experts, neither to which the author lays claim, successive generations of iPods offered additional value in terms of accessories (such as carrying cases and remote) and special features, limited-editions, laser-engraved, autographed iPods from rock stars were also released. Henceforth such improvements and limited edition issues are omitted from the narrative, without detracting from the innovations that each generation represents. Any omissions and errors, technical or otherwise are regretted.

The third generation of the iPod was released in five hard disk sizes - 10 GB, 15GB, 20GB, 30 GB and 40 GB sizes. The iPods themselves were slightly thinner, smaller and lighter. They had a bottom connector port (the *dock connector*) substituting the earlier top mounted FireWire port. However the most telling innovation at around that time was not the iPod itself, but the iTunes Music Store (iTMS). Apple announced this online music store on the same day as the release of the third generation, on 28 April 2003. Individual songs could be downloaded from the iTMS site at less than a penny less $1 a song. This was a big jump over its rivals, given that it created exclusivity in use, locking customers who downloaded the music to the iPod which was the only player that could play the songs[15].

Table 6.1. Major features and main incremental innovations[16]

Generation	Major features and main incremental innovations
1st	Ease of Use (with just one hand). Rotating.. Shuffle, repeat, start-up volume, sleep timer and menus in multiple languages; FireWire port (30 times faster than USB-based players). 10 hours of continuous music. Recharges automatically whenever iPod is connected to a Mac. Ability to download and store contact lists. Could be engraved.
2nd	Touch sensitive immobile wheel. FireWire port had a cover. Laser engraving: $49 (two lines of text with up to 27 characters per line).
3rd	Dock Connector. Middle row of buttons. Fast and easy connection to a computer or stereo. Could build a playlist on iPod. Available in USB ports. Engraving possible ($19). Separate USB 2.0 cable.
4th	*Click Wheel* (for one handed navigation). Colour display with photo viewer replaced monochrome display in October 2004. 12 hours battery life (updated later for 15 hours). Could import photos from digital camera directly into iPod photo.
5th	Slimmer design. Larger screen with video player and lyrics support. The September 2006 enhanced version featured a brighter display. Longer video battery life. New, redesigned earphones included. Album artwork and photos. Plays video: music videos, video Podcasts, home movies and television shows and short films.

In January 2004, Apple introduced a flash disk based player, the iPod mini. It had 4 GB of storage (manufactured by Hitachi) and carried a price of $250. The mini came in five colours of anodized aluminium. Despite being expensive for the amount of music it could hold, the iPod mini proved to be a big success. The same year in July, the fourth generation of

---

[15] The downloaded music can be played in up to five computers and an unlimited amount of iPods can play the files.

[16] Sources: Wikipedia and www.apple.com/pr/library/

the iPod was released. Other than (by now customary and expected) improvements in terms of hard disk space (the 20 GB version were priced at $300 while the 40GB at $400. Comparing this to the previous generation (third) other improvements included a click wheel design from the iPod mini, a colour display and a battery that claimed to run for 12 hours.

The fifth generation[17] came out in October of 2005. Once again, it was in storage capacity which saw the most significant improvements. For the price of the 4th generation 20 GB version, one could buy the 30GB version and similarly the price for the 60 GB 5th generation had the same price tag as the 40GB 4th generation iPod. Other differences of the 5th over the previous generation included the capability to watch movies. In the five generations of the iPod, improvements over previous generations have systematically been in storage (and to some extent battery life) with other marginal improvements principally in design and 'user friendly' aspects of the player.

Table 6.2 presents a *value* variable as measured by dollars per gigabyte as well as an innovation variable, measured by the megabytes per ounce of weight. Note that each 5 GB has a storage capacity of around 1000 songs. In terms of photos, (available since the 4th generation iPod), a 60GB iPod has available storage space for around 25000 photos. A 5th generation 60GB iPod has available space for around 150 hours of video; with the 80GB iPod capable of holding 100 hours of video.

Tables 6.3 and 6.4 contain similar value and innovation calculations as in the previous table, but for other iPod products, namely the iPod mini, iPod shuffle, iPod nano and other special editions. Besides these products, Apple regularly makes media splashes with other iPod variants[18].

---

[17]The product life, as measured by the time between successive generations has approximately been a bit over one year, with the annual reincarnation of the iPod an eagerly awaited spectacle. The 1st and 2nd generations enjoyed a product life of 9 months with 15 months for the 3rd and 4th generations.

[18] For instance, in June 2005, it launched a free recycling campaign, where costumers had a 10% discount when they buy a new one. In March 2006, Apple announced a new software enabling users to set a personal maximum volume limit for their iPods (which could be locked by parents, using a combination code). In October 2006, Apple announced a special edition of iPod nano, created by Bono (U2 lead singer) and Bobby Shriver help the fight against AIDS in Africa, with a portion of the profits reverting for funding programs for African women and children affected by HIV/AIDS.

Table 6.2. The incarnations of the iPod[19] – value and innovation measures

Generation	Size (GB)	Price ($)	Product life[20]	GB/$	GB/ ounce
1st (Oct 23, 2001)	5	399	5 months	79,8	0,77
1st (Mar 2002)	10	499	4 months	49,9	1,54
2nd (Jul 2002)	5	299	9 months	59,8	0,77
	10	399		39,9	1,54
	20	499		24,95	2,78
3rd (April 2003)	10	299	5 months	29,9	1,79
	15	399		26,6	2,68
	30	499		16,63	4,84
3rd (Sep 2003)[21]	10	299	10 months	29,9	1,79
	20	399		19,95	3,57
	40	499		12,475	6,45
4th (Jul 2004)	20	299	3 months	14,95	3,57
	40	399		9,975	6,45
4th iPod photo (Oct 2004)	40	499	4 months	12,475	6,25
	60	599		9,98	9,38
4th iPod photo (Feb 2005)	30	349	4 months	11,63	4,69
	60	449		7,48	9,38
5th (Oct, 2005)	30	299	11 months	9,97	6,25
	60	399		6,65	10,91
5th (Sep 2006)	80	349		4,3625	14,55

[19] Calculated using different sources. For these and additional information, consult www.apple.com/pr/library/

[20] Product life as measured by the time before the release of the next generation of the iPod.

[21] This version was updated just one month later with a free which added support for new voice recording and photo storage accessories, allowing users to record over 600 hours of lectures, interviews or notes (40GB iPod), stored in WAV file format, easily edited and even sent via email. It had a microphone and 16mm speaker and capacity for over 20,000 digital photos from a 3 megapixel camera.

Table 6.3. Major features and main incremental innovations of other iPod products[22]

Generation	Major features and main incremental innovations
iPod mini	5 possible colors: silver, gold, pink, blue or green. Touch-sensitive *Click Wheel* for easy one-handed navigation. Battery capacity about 18 hours.
iPod nano	Ultra-portable, thinner than a standard #2 pencil. Tubes in pink, purple, blue, green. Capacity to view photo slideshows or play games in full color. About 14 hours of battery life for 1st generation and 24 hours for 2nd generation. 2nd generation available in silver, pink, green, blue and black.
iPod shuffle	Smaller and lighter than *a pack of gum*. Album art while playing music, photo slideshows or play games in full color.
iPod U2	Engraving of U2 band member signatures. Included the single *Vertigo* (new at the time – October 2004). A new one was launched in June 2006, based on 5th generation iPod, with 30 minutes of exclusive U2 video
iPod radio remote	Combination of wired remote control and new FM radio capabilities for iPod nano and fifth generation iPod.
iPod hi-fi	High-fidelity speaker system to redefine the home stereo system. Delivers an acoustic performance and room-filling sound
iPod Nike	Nike+iPod Sport Kit: wireless system allowing iPod nano to be used as a pedometer.
iPod Harry Potter	Harry Potter audiobook series was available exclusively on iTunes. Possibility for fans to purchase a Collector's Edition: a 20GB iPod engraved with the Hogwarts crest.

Apple remains focused in its efforts to innovate and to exploring new markets and applications, for instance connecting with car manufacturers. BMW was the first car maker to release an interface for *iPod automobile*. Apple believes that a majority of US cars would come equipped with the iPod.

Fig 6.1 illustrates the price per gigabyte (left vertical axis) and the quarterly sales evolution (right vertical axis) of successive generations of iPods[23]. The value variable that we have chosen is the price per GB offered by the iPod. The price per GB has continuously fallen from $80 to approximately $4! In the right axis we have the sales of each, reported in the

---

[22] Sources: Wikipedia and www.apple.com/pr/library/

[23] Note that there were months where there was more than one value (i.e. July 02). This is because more than one model was released in that particular month.

quarterly reports. Sales have been steadily increasing on the other hand, with. Q1 2006 sales at over 14 million iPods.

Table 6.4. Other iPod products

Generation/Product	Size (GB)	Price ($)	Product life	GB/$
1st iPod mini (Jan 2004)	4	249	13 months	62,25
2nd iPod mini (Feb 2005)	4	199	7 months	49,75
	6	249		41,5
1st iPod nano (Sep 2005)[24]	2	199	5 months	99,5
	4	249		62,25
1st iPod nano (Feb 2006)	1	149	7 months	149
2nd iPod nano (Set 2006)	2	149		74,5
	4	199		49,75
	8	249		31,125
1st iPod shuffle (Jan 2005)	512 (MB)	99	20 months	198
	1	149		149
1st iPod shuffle (Feb 2006)[25]	512 (MB)	69		138
	1G	99		99
2nd iPod shuffle (Sep 2006)	1	79		79
iPod U2 (Oct 2004)	20	349		17,45
iPod U2 (Jun 2006)	30	329		10,97
iPod radio remote (Jan 2006)		49		
iPod Hi-Fi		349		
iPod Harry Potter		32.95 to 49.95[26]		
		249[27]		
iPod Nike (May 2006)		29		

[24] Substituted iPod mini.
[25] Just price change.
[26] Individual audio books.
[27] Harry Potter Digital Box Set.

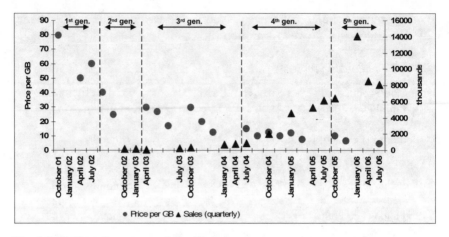

Fig. 6.1. *Dollars for space* and iPod sales

Fig. 6.2 reveals a similar value trend for other iPod products (mini, nano, shuffle and U2). Once again the figure illustrates a decrease in the price per GB.

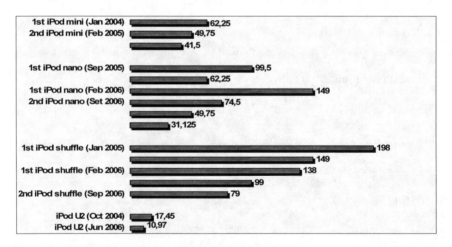

Fig. 6.2. *Dollars for space* for other iPod products

What Figs. 6.1 and 6.2 don't show is that as the price of storage fell, the iPod improved in other ways. They became thinner, got larger displays, longer battery lives, brighter screens and better interfaces as detailed in Table 6.1.

Another measure of innovation that we calculated was the hard disk space per gram of weight (gigabyte per weight, see Table 6.2). This would also represent the number of songs for a given weight of the iPod. As we can see from Fig. 6.3, this value has continuously increased with each new version.

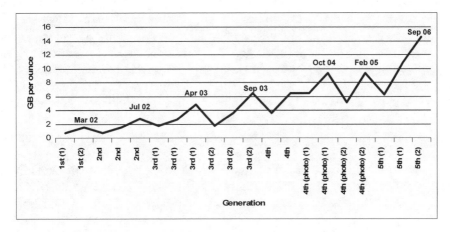

Fig. 6.3. Weight per ounce of successive generations of the iPod

Fig. 6.4 illustrates the sales trends (in absolute terms as well as percentage growth). As we can see, although the growth has been steady, after mid 2006, there has been some slowdown. Only the coming times would tell whether increased competition from the likes of Microsoft Zune or the Samsung Z5 would have any marked effect on iPod's success.

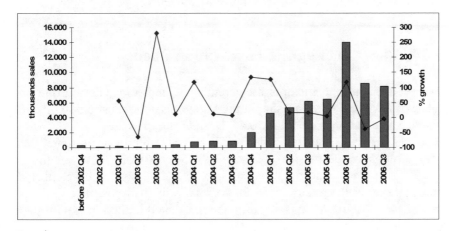

Fig. 6.4. iPod sales and percentage sales growth

Box 6.1: The iPod ecosystem

In the fiscal year of 2006, Apple sold about 39,4 million iPods, or 75 every second. A look at the 2006 Christmas catalogues of leading stores reveal the extent to which stores and not just the manufacturers depending upon the iPod as well as the host of iPod peripherals - the iPod ecosystem. The magazine Fast Company (in August 2005) regards an ecosystem as "...a set of companies, cooperating and competing at once, that together deliver a product or service by providing different components that share some critical capabilities. In an ecosystem, more than one company can provide features or functions to the product."

A New York Times article reported this veritable iPod ecosystem, whereby many firms and not just component suppliers, but also accessory manufacturers live off the success of the iPod (New York Times, 2006/02/03). It was estimated that for every $3 spent on an iPod, at least $1 is spent on an accessory. One survey of teenagers found that 77 percent of teens who owned a music player have an iPod, up from 74 percent of teens in the fall of 2005.

The iPod is also changing people's lifestyles. Thanks to podcasted lectures one can still be at that urgent date, without missing out (to some extent) on class lectures! In 2006, almost 30% of all new cars are reported to have come with iPod integration, some of which would also incorporate voice control capabilities for drivers.

6.3 iPod in the Integrated Innovation Space

The iPod's constant attempts at incremental innovation, despite the absence of any clear rival looming in the horizon, can be illustrated in the integrated innovation space (Fig. 6.4). Despite the existence of MP3 based products during its launch, as discussed earlier the iPod was presented as a breakthrough in the musical experience, clearly a wolf. However the 1st and 2nd generations had small market outcome (as measured by number of units sold as well as market share), perhaps principally because they just ran on Mac. In Fig. 6.4 this situation is represented in the integrated space by the positions marked **1** and **2,** denoting also the respective generations. The bigger innovation jump of iPod appeared in April 2003, with the release of the 3rd generation iPod: with more storage capacity than previous versions, and also with the ability to run on Mac and PC's. With this, iPod conquered something about 58% of market share in the digital music market (**3**).

The continuous improvements both in the ease of use as well as characteristics of successive versions of the iPod boosted the market, share even further, shown by shifts outward of the payoff curve outwards in the strategy space (second quadrant.) Although data on margins are hard to come by, we opted to depict two variables in the outcome space - market share and margins. Shifts outward of the curve relating these two variables imply an increase in the number of units sold or production and distribution efficiency improvements. It is believed that currently margins in the order of about 20 to 25 percent, revealing possibilities of scale economies.

Apple's iPod has dominated the portable audio market so overwhelmingly that that giants like Sony, Dell, Microsoft were left scratching their heads wondering how best to come up with a strong contender. Digital song sales however account for only about 5 percent of the overall music market iPod maintains its overwhelming dominance in the MP3 business Despite some hiccups along the way, the sale of iPods has risen consistently (with a small dip in the fall of 2006). Just six months about the first millionth unit sold, iPod sales hit the 2 million mark. In January 2004 Apple launched the iPod mini, with 4GB capacity and in five colours. Demand was so high that Apple had to delay the launch of iPod mini abroad. Four months after reaching the second million unit sales, iPod reaches the third[28].

Fig. 6.5 plots the continuous attempts at incremental innovation of the five generations of the iPod, in the integrated innovation space. The outcome space incorporates two outcome dimensions - market share and margins. While reliable figures on margins are hard to come by (especially since the margin depends both on the period as well as the version) we relied on technology blogs for the figures.

---

[28] At the same time, the number of songs sold via iTunes reached a historic milestone: one hundred million songs! In the same year the library of songs reached 1 million available songs.

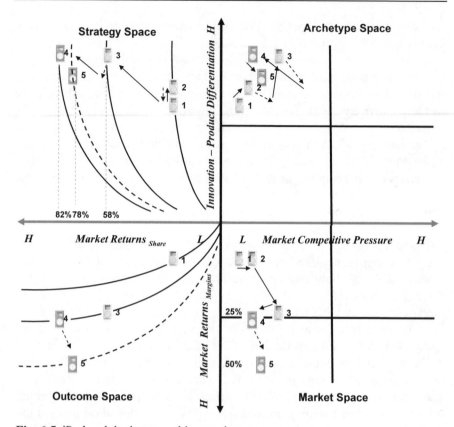

Fig. 6.5. iPod and the integrated innovation space

During October of 2006, analysts reported that iPod sales accounted for somewhere around 82% of all digital music players (creative ran second with a measly 3.7% share). It was also in October 2006 that iPod launched its 4th generation model (marked **4** in Fig. 6.5). This version of the iPod (as discussed in the previous section) marked even further and margins hovered around 20 to 25 percent[29].

Position 5 in the figure is suggestive of the future position in the integrated space. Reports speculate that the fifth generation margins are expected to reach to about 50%, linked to the continuous decline of prices of hard disk drives[30].

---

[29] Some of these details were culled from the quarterly conference calls and can be seen at the site http://macminute.com.

[30] See, for example, http://www.ipodnn.com/articles/05/09/22/ipod.nano.margins/ or http://www.appleinsider.com/article.php?id=2052.

Early iPods had a clear form factor and ease of use advantages over their competitors. Nowadays, though, the hardware competition has become much stronger, particularly in the *mini* segment that's seeing strong growth. The changes that we've seen since the debut of the iPod have mostly been refinements — thinner designs, colour screens, smaller form factors, shuffled controls, and tweaked interfaces.

The strongest competition to the iPod may yet come from a newcomer, Microsoft's Zune released in November of 2006. Although other contenders exist (Dell, Creative, iRiver, Samsung to name a few), the software giant's challenge to iPod hegemony is the clearest. Similarities are also pronounced with both the 30GB Zune priced similarly to the iPod 30GB video at $250, with Microsoft also planning to sell songs via its Zune marketplace for $1 apiece—the same price Apple charges for songs via its iTunes Store. Zune comes with a built in FM player that iPod doesn't have except via add-ons. Whether this would be sufficient to knock iPod of its pedestal, only time will tell.

Zune has some features not included in iPod. Besides the FM player early referred, Zune as also a wireless connection to other Zune devices, to share songs. Early indications are that Zune has made a positive impact in the MP3 market, capturing 9% in the first week of the release but soon slipped to the fifth position (December 8, 2006), accounting for a little over 3% of the MP3 market (tying with Disney which sells a line of kid friendly MP3 players).

Box 6.2: Applying other people's ideas!

A killer application such as the iPod, based on existing technology is not completely new. History is replete with cases of original inventions that generated little or no returns to their original inventors but were successfully applied by others.

Thomas Edison has often been wrongly credited for inventing the light bulb. The incandescent filament bulb and its predecessor, the arc light, were around for about 50 years prior to Edison's design. He improved upon the invention making it practical for home use and together with his electric power distribution model, Edison was able to harness and gain from the invention.

(continued)

Box 6.2: Applying other people's ideas! (cont.)

At Zerox´s Palo Alto Research Center (PARC) were churned out many of the standard elements of today's computing. Indeed one of the first personal computers was developed there (the Xerox Alto), much before Apple or IBM. PARC developed breakthrough inventions such as the graphical user interface (GUI), a word processing software, a workstation, a laser printer, a local area network and the hand-held mouse. Yet Xerox was unable to profit from any of these.

The story of AT&T is similar to that of Xerox, where in 1947 AT&T laboratories created the first transistor in the world. Unable to capitalize on their invention, in 1952 AT&T decided to license out the transistor. For $ 25.000 firms such as Texas Instruments, Sony and IBM acquired a technology that would produce billions of revenues (http://innovationzen.com/blog/2006/07/26/invention-vs-innovation).

Much of the genius lies not so much in the invention, but on capitalizing on it. This is how Amazon which didn't invent retailing nor eBay which didn't invent auctions nor Microsoft which didn't invent the GUI, were able to become the giants they are today.

7 Staying Alive: Struggles in Innovation Space

Well now, I get low and I get high
And if I can't get either I really try.
Got the wings of heaven on my shoes
I'm a dancin' man and I just can't lose.
You know it's all right, it's O.K.
I'll live to see another day

From the lyrics of *Staying Alive*

7.1 Innovation: Staying Alive

While commoditization is an ever omnipresent threat, many established firms see the future of their industry not in terms of commoditization, but of impending irrelevance. Today's icons are increasingly being thrust aside by new firms and new products. This decline of erstwhile industry dominance need not arise due to disruptive innovations that seen earlier in Chap. 2 and in Chap. 5[1]. Rather, the discussion in this chapter is the struggle that some leaders face, in thwarting of challenges from upstarts. A struggle oftentimes to stay relevant.

Three cases best illustrate this striving to stay relevant - two in the toy industry and the third in the browser industry. In this chapter we present the cases of LEGO building bricks, Barbie dolls and of the browser wars. The first is the story of LEGO toys, which have a long and illustrious history stretching back more than seventy years, presented in Sect. 7.2. In that section we sketch a brief history of the major improvements of the toy maker, whose attempts at incremental innovation in the approximately sixty years (more than seventy if one takes into account the early wooden toys of the founder) of the history of the LEGO Group.

---

[1] Recall from our discussion earlier, disruptive innovations are due to the emergence of new products some of whose attributes are worse than those of the incumbent product, but leads to the failure of leading firms in an industry.

In Sect. 7.3, we observe how Barbie, an icon of the doll industry, much like LEGO, is also struggling to stay alive in the imagination and attention of young girls. Unlike LEGO though, Barbie faces a more direct threat from a new competitor. Both LEGO and Barbie have their legions of followers and collectors. And today both are trying to still be relevant. In either case one is hard-pressed to come up with evidence of a consistent pattern of strategic errors. We use the Integrated Model to try to trace out the struggles of LEGO and Barbie in the integrated innovation space.

The third case we present in this chapter is that of the struggles of Netscape in what has come to be termed as the *browser wars*. The jostling of firms for market leadership in a competitive environment is best illustrated by web browsers. Sect. 7.4 follows the dramatic rise and fall of Netscape with the accompanying rise of Microsoft's Internet Explorer. Once again, we use actual data to show the dynamics of the browser wars, applying the Integrated Model. The case of the browser wars hold important lessons for firms today as the digital business landscape becomes ever more important, both for traditional firms as well as those that are purely web based.

7.2 Innovation in Toy Land – The LEGO Story

The name LEGO, is derived from the Danish *Leg Godt* meaning *play well*, is synonymous with high quality plastic toy bricks. Marrying these building bricks with a child's imagination allows myriad construction of anything from houses to ships to cars. However, today the world's oldest and most successful toy company, that has spawned everything from fan clubs to theme parks, is struggling to stay alive. LEGO is endeavouring to o remain relevant in a market place that is increasingly dominated by a digital play world of online games and hand held consoles.

LEGO has its origins in small wooden toys created by a carpenter in Denmark.[2] The first plastic bricks were produced by the LEGO Group in 1949[3]. Developed in the spirit of the earlier wooden bricks, they could be

---

[2] Interested readers are advised to visit LEGO's official site and Wikipedia for more on LEGO's history. These two sites have been the major sources for research used in this section Another interesting site devoted entirely to information about LEGO is Brickwiki (www.brickwiki.org) an open content LEGO encyclopaedia!

[3] The LEGO bricks were based on an existing product. In 1947, LEGO's founder and his son obtained samples of interlocking plastic bricks produced by a

stacked upon one another and interlocked. However it was only nine years later, in 1958 that the current brick design was developed, built on the concept of the *LEGO System*. This was based on a system of creative play, replacing the earlier *Automatic Binding Bricks*. The interlocking characteristic of the plastic bricks[4] was vastly improved as was their versatility.

In the following year, 1959, the genesis of a research and development centre the *Futura* division, was created. This centre was entrusted with the task of generating ideas for new LEGO sets. *Futura* was to play a pivotal role in both and product development and exploring new applications of the LEGO Group over the following decades.

The years 1961 and 1962 saw the introduction of the first LEGO wheels, an addition that expanded the potential for building cars, trucks, buses and other vehicles based on the LEGO bricks. Today LEGO is one of the largest tire manufacturers in the world! In 1964 LEGO sets came with instruction manuals which were included with the sets. A couple of years later, the LEGO train system, was released which was to later prove to be one of the most popular LEGO product ever.

In 1969, the *Duplo* system was introduced, which was exactly twice the size of the regular building brick. The *Duplo* was aimed at younger children was also compatible with the regular building bricks. Further product improvements and expansion of the product line occurred in the following years, including targeting specifically at the market for girls as well as the release of the *LEGO family*.

The increasing popularity of LEGO products among adults, led the company to begin to exploit a more adult market niche towards the mid 1970s. The year 1977 saw the release of the *Expert Builder* Series sets, an improvement of the Expert Series which had been released two years earlier. These technical sets featured moving parts such as gears, levers, axles etc. permitting the construction for instance, of realistic cars. In 1979, the

---

company called Kiddicraft which manufactured interlocking bricks. In 1949 under the LEGO Group manufacturing commenced of similar bricks called "Automatic Binding Bricks."

[4] The basic LEGO brick has a length of 32 mm and a width of 16 mm and 9,5 mm high, and is often referred to as "the 2 by 4 inch building brick", "the LEGO eight-knob brick " or "the 2 x 4 brick" (due to the two rows of four bosses each). Since 1958, the name "LEGO" has been inscribed on the top surface of each boss. Its dimensions are the only aspect of the brick which has not been subject to a patent.

introduction of the smiling yellow LEGO mini-figure brought humans into LEGO creations. Succeeding years saw further product line expansion with the creation of sets based on the space theme.

1982 saw the morphing of The *Expert Builder* series into the *Technic* series and a year later the *Duplo* system expanded to include sets for infants. Light & Sound sets which added an element of realism made their first appearance in 1986. It was in that year too that the Technic Computer Control was introduced which enabled the control of Technic motorized models including robots, to be controlled using a computer.

In 1998, LEGO launched Mindstorms, programmable LEGO bricks. Called the LEGO Mindstorms Robotic Invention Kit and priced at $200, it consisted of 717 pieces including traditional LEGO bricks, motors, gears, sensors, and an *RCX Brick* with an embedded microprocessor. Mindstorms enabled the construction of various LEGO robotic creations both by children as well as adults and proved to be an instant success.

In 1999 in partnership with Lucas Film Ltd., LEGO launched fourteen *Star Wars*-themed kits. These Star Wars kits proved to be the biggest sellers in LEGO´s history. Children were not just assembling characters that they could recognize from the Star Wars sequel of movies, but could also play out scenes from the movies.

In 2001 the company released another product which also proved to be commercially very successful - a world of action figures known as *Bionicle*. A combination of the words 'biological' and *chronicle*, a story line was created where the Bionicle figures consisting of six heroes, six small wise people and five villains inhabited a tropical island called Mata Nui. The legend has been elaborately crafted with each category of Bionicle and each character possessing a name with the designs suggesting personalities. Innovation for LEGO means not just creating now product lines, but creating imaginary theatres for the products to play their roles!

7.2.1 Staying Alive

In the world of toys, LEGO has come a long way from simple artisanal wooden toys to today's wide range of the LEGO Group, from the *Duplo* for infants to sophisticated modular building sets to robots. In the process, LEGO has also tried to cater to a wide range of age groups, from the *Duplo* for infants to robots for adults.

As we have seen, the LEGO Group's strategy has been to come up with ever more offerings no longer confined to just toys. LEGO has built sophisticated computer games (which it later abandoned) and theme parks. Indeed LEGO Group is coming up with a range of products running the entire gamut of diversion for kids as well as trying to exploit an adult niche. The recent expansion of LEGO product lines from the Star Wars kits to *Bionicle* and Harry Potter sets has led LEGO to the creation of ongoing LEGO characters with which children can identify. When the script was missing, LEGO supplied it as has been the case of the *Bionicle*. But despite the huge loyalty that LEGO products command and the passion that it inspires, the LEGO Group is struggling commercially. This despite one of the most powerful brand recognition in the world and despite being acknowledged by both *Fortune* and *Forbes* magazines who named LEGO as the toy of the 20th century[5].

LEGO is competing not just with similar products of other companies[6], but with other instruments of diversion and distraction. It is in a battlefield that includes TV, video games, computers and the internet. LEGO's fight is of trying to stay relevant.

From its core legacy, the basic brick, LEGO has constantly tried to innovate, not as much in the product per se, but in exploring the myriad applications that the interlocking brick permits. LEGO Group's greatest innovation was and still remains *clutch power* which permits two LEGO pieces when snapped together to stay in place[7].

---

[5] See Fast Company (2001).

[6] Over the years LEGO has faced a number of direct competitors, several of whom have interlocking toy building bricks that are nearly identical to the LEGO bricks. Best-Lock, Tyco toys (owned by Mattel Inc) and Mega Bloks are three of the major competitors that eagerly fight for market shares on the toy construction market.

[7] This clutch power is gives great versatility to LEGO products. This coupling power enabled LEGO to constantly create new figures, themes and applications, all based on the LEGO bricks which combined with imagination allows the construction of any number of models.

Box 7.1: LEGO to user led innovation

LEGO is also leading the way in tapping its consumers for innovation. Recent trends suggest that Lego is an excellent illustration of what von Hippel (2005) calls user led innovation. As quoted in an article from the New York Times, entitled *"To Charge Up Costumers, Put Costumers in Charge"* (18th June, 2006):

"It's getting cheaper and cheaper for users to innovate on their own. This is not traditional market research — asking customers what they want. This is identifying what your most advanced users are already doing and understanding what their innovations mean for the future of your business."

Lego *Digital Designer* tool allows anybody to design anything based on Lego bricks. Users can then order the bricks which they can then use to construct their virtual designs. User based innovation has had a pivotal role in the 2006 release of the *Mindstorms* robotic kit (see Wired magazine's February 2006 article – *"Geeks in Toyland"*, which recounts the fascinating tale of how some Lego fans were recruited, without pay, to help design the 3rd version of Mindstorms!) Wanting to make a clean break from the past, the third Mindstorms version was to give back the ease of use of Lego creations to children. A majority of Mindstorms robots have been constructed by adults, an unintended consequence of Mindstorm's success and the complexity of the robotic creation also had a part to play in that. Lego created a Mindstorms User Panel (MUP) that helped with the design of Mindstorms NXT (as the new release is called) and was critical to the success of the robot creation in 20 minutes, a goal of the new release.

7.2.2 Staying Alive in the Archetype Space

The struggle to stay alive is illustrated in the integrated innovation space in Fig. 7.1 below. Starting from an innovative wolf, the increasing availability of other products appealing to the child's (and adults) diversion time including playstations, television, computer games and the internet, have all led LEGO to loose the appeal it once had. It finds itself squarely in fox territory. This horizontal gravitational pull to the fox territory has implied that the LEGO group has to constantly come up with increasing applications and new product spin-offs, as discussed in this section. All this (like coming up with *Bionicle* sets and the *Mindstorms* robotic kit) LEGO's struggle are the attempts to differentiate itself and inch as close to the wolf territory as possible, to increase market share. This product differentiation strategy has been coupled with efforts at cost reduction (this dynamic is not shown but would appear in the outcome space described by market share and margins).

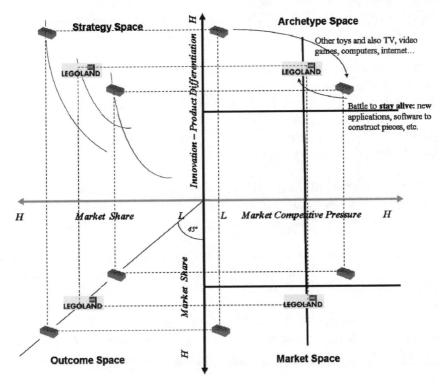

Fig. 7.1. LEGO staying alive

7.3 Staying Alive II: Barbie

Barbie looked upon as an icon of childhood by millions of women while reviled by others, is the world's best selling doll. She was released in 1959 by Mattel Inc. as a personal project of Ruth Handler, cofounder of the company. Like the interlocking bricks of LEGO, a teenage doll in itself is not new, the model being based on a doll in Germany[8]. Just as LEGO,

---

[8] Lilli, a German doll was based on a cartoon strip in a German newspaper. Ruth Handler bought a doll during a trip to Switzerland with her daughter, named Barbie. She took it back with her to the impress upon the management of Mattel

Barbie is also struggling to stay alive in the imagination and attention of young girls. Like LEGO but more intensely, Barbie is facing a direct challenge from an upstart. In this section, we briefly review the history of Barbie and the strategy of expansion of product line-her myriad persona. We then witness the emerging threat from a competitor and the strategic manoeuvres of both products. Finally the struggle to stay relevant and alive is put in the context of the integrated innovation space.

When discussing innovation and product differentiation, it is perhaps important to ask how does one 'innovate' on a doll, whose personality is already determined? Mattel Inc.'s. response has been to create a multi faceted, multi profession, multi look doll. Innovation takes the form not of product improvement, but rather of proliferation. That is to say, Barbie is not one doll; she is many, with some essential characteristics.

The first Barbie doll wore a black-and-white zebra-striped swimsuit and signature topknot ponytail crowned either as blonds or brunettes. However in succeeding years[9] Barbie donned other hair styles and colours.

As tastes and fashion and social mores changed, so did Barbie. In the same life (she never ages), Barbie has had a variety of incarnations and a variety of careers. One count[10] gave Barbie forty two careers, ranging from a ballerina, to a rock star to the President of the United States! While the cofounder of Mattel, Ruth Handler, the person who discovered Barbie, died in 2002 at the age of 85, Barbie is still alive. Still young and still beautiful. In fact she never grew up!

Besides the splintering of the Barbie persona and the associated toys and dolls that this splintering permitted, the Barbie brand personified in movies as well, starting with Barbie in the Nutcracker in 2001. A worldwide success, three other movies were produced in each succeeding year.

The incessant search for accessory spin offs has created a veritable Barbie ecosystem (sprung by Mattel) associated with Barbie's varied and evolving lifestyle. Thus Barbie had thirty eight different pets, from cats to dogs to a panda and even a zebra. Possessing a driver's license meant she had to have cars from pink convertibles to trailers. And of course she has

---

Inc. that an adult doll was a good idea. Ruth had not realized that the eleven and half inch doll was a sex toy for German men!

[9] Source: Wikipedia.

[10] The multifaceted and career Barbie is described in the Wikipedia.

friends, a family and even a boy friend, Ken, estranged for some time but now united!

7.3.1 The Battle of the Dolls

While Barbie has the same problem as LEGO, in terms of vying for compete for a child's attention, there is an added twist as Barbie's efforts to stay alive has acquired a more urgent note posing a direct threat to Barbie. This has been due to a new entrant in the fashion doll industry, in the form of Bratz. The toymaker MGA Entertainment introduced four new dolls on the block, the Bratz in the summer of 2001. The new fashion dolls came in different skin tones, with pouting, street-smart expressions wearing trendy outfits[11].

The Bratz dolls seemed more adept at keeping with the times, proving to be a hit in the United States and other countries capturing and staying in the number one fashion doll spot for three years. In the year of its launch in 2001, Bratz had revenues of $100 million. By the end of 2004 the Bratz brand had revenues of more than $3 billion, including hundreds of licensed products ranging from bicycles to computers[12].

As noted by a Barbie researcher Fara Warner, there are many factors that can be attributed to Bratz's success at the cost of Barbie. As she noted:

> "If Barbie® were a real woman, she would stand 6 foot 2 and most likely would be unable to stand because of her tiny waist and large bust. By contrast, if Bratz™ were real girls, they would stand about 5 foot 6 and sport bodies that look more like entertainers … In addition, the Bratz™ dolls display none of the 'role modelling' Barbie® did for decades. "Bratz™ don't have careers per se, or at least their clothes don't reflect that. Instead, the dolls' clothing and accessories are knockoffs of the fashions young girls see—and want—in the real world or on channels such as MTV and BET. The girls decide what they want their dolls to be when they grow up or if they just want to hang out and try on clothes. There was no rule book on what was appropriate for these young girls, no role model of what they should be or shouldn't be."

---

[11] The four Bratz dolls are Yasmin, Jade, Sasha and Cloe. For a fuller discussion on the emergence of the Bratz threat, read the chapter entitled *Toppling Barbie: Bratz Predict the Future*, Warner (2005). The chapter is available at http://www.thepowerofthepurse.com/Warner_CH08.pdf.

[12] Source: Ibid.

There have been some missteps in Mattel´s response including a slow response due to internal challenges such as the acquisition of the Learning Company distracting management as well as its disinclination to change its key product[13]. However Mattel seems to be fighting back, and if imitation is the sincerest form of flattery, then Bratz must have been flattered with Mattel coming up with several *Bratz Fighters.* This took for instance in the form of *My Scene Barbie,* who had more fashionable clothes, released in December of 2002. A year later a group of dolls came out from Mattel's with ethnic looks and urban fashions inspired by Bratz. Mattel also started creating dolls based on the winners of the highly successful American Idol television contest in February 2004. Drama and excitement was created with Ken, Barbie's boyfriend for 43 years split up, only to reunite two years later in February of 2006!

Box 7.2: Annual sale – toy industry in the US

Video games represent a ferocious competitor of traditional toys. From the following table we can see that while: video games' sales grew 6% in 2005, traditional toys witnessed a decrease in their sales. Dolls were one of the categories which saw a decrease (2%). Interesting is the remarkable growth of building sets, which includes the fight back of LEGO.

Table Box 7.2. US Toy Industry Sales

Category	$ Toy Sales 2005 (USD)	% Change from Prior Year
Action Figures and Accessories	$1.3 billion	4%
Arts and Crafts	$2.4 billion	-4%
Building Sets	$695.2 million	16%

Source: The NPD Group February 2006

(continued)

Box 7.2: Annual sale – toy industry in the US (cont.)

---

[13] Ibid.

Table Box 7.2a. US Toy Industry Sales (cont.)

Category	$ Toy Sales 2005 (USD)	% Change from Prior Year
Dolls	$2.7 billion	-2%
Games/Puzzles	$2.4 billion	-9%
Infant and Preschool	$3.1 billion	-1%
Learning and Exploration	$392.0 million	5%
Outdoor and Sports Toys	$2.7 billion	-3%
Plush	$1.3 billion	-15%
Vehicles	$1.8 billion	-8%
All Other Toys	$2.5 billion	-4%
Total Traditional Toy Industry	*$21.3 billion*	*-4%*
Total Video Games	*$10.5 billion*	*6%*

Source: The NPD Group February 2006

Not surprisingly, there is a big divergence in the preference for toys among boys and girls. According to the 2006 data released by the National Retail Foundation of the USA, T.M.X. Elmo (in its tenth year) is the must have toy for boys while Barbie remains the queen among girls! Table Box 7.2b below gives the top ten toy preference for boys and girls as reported by the retail foundation.

Table Box 7.2b. Toy preferences by gender

Top toys for Boys	Top toys for Girls
T.M.X. Elmo	Barbie
Cars (generic)	Dolls (generic)
PlayStation 3	Bratz
Video Games	T.M.X. Elmo
LEGO	Dora the Explorer
Nintendo DS	Disney Princess
Hot Wheels	iPod/MP3 Players
Xbox 360	Nintendo DS
Remote controlled cars	PlayStation 3
Trucks	The Little Mermaid

Source: National Retail Foundation (USA)

Other initiatives that were part of Mattel´s arsenal of the Barbie fight-back included partnering with top fashion designers to create an adult collection, story telling and even live Barbie shows. The way all this plays out in the children's must have list could very well determine the continual survival of Barbie or spell the demise of a cultural icon.

7.3.2 Fighting Back in the Integrated Space

Once again, the integrated innovation space provides the background to illustrate the fight for market share in the *doll wars*. Barbie, to a large extent had been a wolf till the end of the 20th century, branding, history and consumer loyalty all playing an important role in this. The advent of Bratz has marked a decline in her reign, along with other forms of entertainment. Bratz is currently fighting out with Barbie in the fox territory with Bratz holding the upper hand when it comes to market appeal.

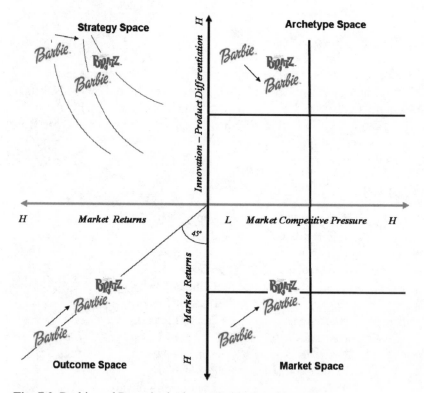

Fig. 7.2. Barbie and Bratz in the integrated innovation space

In the outcome space, market returns are suggestive of actual positions.

7.4 Browser Wars – From Mosaic to Netscape to Explorer to ...Firefox?

The internet provides an interesting battleground that illustrates the jostling among firms for market leadership in a very competitive environment. An environment where traffic is one of the principal metrics of success, with immediate financial returns non existent. The history of the browser wars illustrates one such case of bitter fighting for market dominance.

In this section we follow the dramatic rise and consequent fall of the Netscape browser. A fall that inversely mirrors the dramatic rise of the Microsoft Internet Explorer. The case of the browser wars, unlike LEGO and Barbie, is not an issue of struggling to remain relevant. The competition for dominance in the web browser marketplace holds important lessons for the 21st century firm, as the digital business landscape becomes ever more important. And this digital playground can prove to be a battleground where today's ruler is tomorrow's has been.

Although the World Wide Web (www) was invented in 1991 the first browser not exclusive to the scientific community was the Mosaic 1.0[14]. Released in November of 1993, it supported images and was developed by the NCSA (National Council for Supercomputer Applications) a research institute at the University of Illinois.

The month of December of the following year saw the release of the Netscape browser (created by members of the Mosaic development team). Netscape improved on Mosaic's usability and reliability. The Netscape browser quickly captured a significant part of the nascent market. By 1995 Netscape towered over the browser market, accounting for approximately 55% of the market, with most of the remainder falling under Mosaic territory[15]. Netscape pursued a strategy of offering free *evaluation copies* of the browser which were downloadable, helping enormously its early adoption (see Box 7.2 for a brief history of the internet and the pre Netscape era browsers).

By the mid 1990s with ever more people going online, Microsoft was waking up to the promises of the internet. In August of 1995 it released the

---

[14] For an early history of browsers, read http://www.quirksmode.org/browsers/ history.html.

[15] Although data on browser shares prior to 1996 is not very reliable, wikipedia does an excellent job in data compilation from different sources for this period.

Internet Explorer 1.0 (IE 1.0) bundled as part of the Microsoft Windows 95 *Plus Pack*. A few months later, in November of 1995, it released the IE 2.0. Both these versions were licensed from (Spyglass Enhanced) Mosaic.

A year after Microsoft's entry, Netscape came up with the final version of Netscape 2.0 in March of 1996 followed quickly by Netscape 3.0 in August 1996. Both Netscape 2.0 and 3.0 marked important improvements, with version 2.0 supporting frames and JavaScript while version 3.0 supported *mouseovers* and some other features[16]. In 1996, slightly more than 80% of the internet users used Netscape. By then the original Mosaic browser was well on its way to decline. NCSA finally stopped developing the Mosaic in January of 1997 since by then both Netscape and Microsoft (which had licensed the Mosaic till then) had their own development teams working on their proprietary browsers.

A bit after the mid 1990s, with the internet really taking off, (see Fig.7.3) Microsoft started seriously investing in its own web browsers. In August 1996, it came up with the Internet Explorer 3.0 posing the first real challenge to Netscape's browser dominance. This version of the browser was the first to support Cascading Style Sheets (CSS), which enabled styling in HTML, making web pages even more popular.

Unlike Netscape which had been charging a small sum from the user, Microsoft allowed free download of IE. At that time though, the IE was still way behind Netscape in popularity, accounting for approximately 3.75% of the browser market share compared to Netscape's 80% share. However a combination of sharp marketing strategy and enhanced features[17] the browser share of the Explorer started steadily rising. By 1997, with hindsight, it appears that Netscape still did not see the looming threat. Despite a small drop in its share to 72.5% it still had a commanding lead over the Internet Explorer 3.0, which had increased its share more than

---

[16] Considered an innovation was the documents array through which one could change images on the web page thus creating the mouseover effect. This effect was enabled when holding the computer mouse over any web screen object that was an active link, with text appearing next to the pointer. This is now a standard on all browsers.

[17] This included making the browser ever friendlier to the increasing of non-'geeks' users the internet.

four fold to 17.5%. Microsoft used its dominance of the Windows operating systems to telling effect, bundling[18] it with the Internet Explorer.

Microsoft released the 4th incarnation of the Internet Explorer in October 97, a few months after the release of Netscape 4.0. Many felt that IE 4.0 marked the beginning of the emergence of Microsoft's browser superiority[19].

Microsoft held a release party for the IE 4.0 which featured a ten-foot-tall letter "*e*" logo. The following telling incident the day after the release party in San Francisco, is recounted in the Wikipedia, at a time when the Netscape corporation was still basking in its browser dominance:

> "Netscape employees showing up to work the following morning found that giant logo on their front lawn, with a sign attached which read "From the IE team." The Netscape employees promptly knocked it over and set a giant figure of their Mozilla dragon mascot atop it, holding a sign reading "Netscape 72, Microsoft 18" (representing the market distribution)."

That was perhaps the proverbial last hurrah for Netscape.

A couple of years later, the 'browser wars' were declared over. Internet consultants, *WebSide Story*, had the following story in 1999. *Browser War All But Over* ran the headline which went on to say:

> "Microsoft Crushing Netscape, Takes 3-to-1 Lead SAN DIEGO, CA -- August 9, 1999 – *WebSideStory* (http: //www .websidestorycom), the leading provider of Internet tracking and traffic analysis, today reported that Microsoft's Internet Explorer has increased its lead of browser users to a dominant 3-to-1 ratio…"

---

[18] A majority of internet users liked the convenience of not having to download and install a browser on their personal computers. In 1996. the US Justice Department investigated claims made by Netscape Communications Corp. that Microsoft pressured PC makers into bundling IE with systems.

[19] One widely respected tech journal had the following to say about the IE4.0. "Let's face it: Microsoft has never been more right in claiming that IE is integral to its OS. True, it might have passed for a separate application in ye olden days of 3.0, but forget about Win 98; IE 4.0 is already one great, big blendo. Worse yet, it's immediately clear that seamless Net integration is appropriate, intelligent, and exactly what you'd desire and demand from an OS circa 1997." *HotWired: NetSurf* (October 27, 1997).

By then Internet Explorer had completely trounced Netscape. The two versions together (both IE 5.0 which had been released in March of 1999, and IE 4.0) accounted for a bit over 75% as compared to a 22% share of Netscape.

It was with IE 4.0 that the tide had started turning for Microsoft. A few factors were instrumental for the dramatic decline of Netscape, (remember the release party incident!), hubris playing a very small part. Microsoft proved superior both in terms of technology as well as marketing strategy based on its vastly superior resources. IE was faster and provided the possibility for truly *dynamic* pages allowing MP3 playback. Netscape despite its prior dominance, was still a relatively small company with a single product, as compared to Microsoft, for whom, the Internet Explorer was not its core product, a non revenue generator. Microsoft's dominance in the operating systems enabled bundling of IE with every copy of Windows. By forcing Netscape to be offered for free (from January of 1998 Netscape had started offering its browser for free), Netscape's revenues were down to a trickle, strangling development budgets.

By the year 2000, the Internet Explorer's share of the browser market stood at a massive 84%. From a 90% share a few years earlier, Netscape's share then stood at 13%. This is a startling story of demise, perhaps one of the most dramatic in an internet landscape littered with the remains of technology start-ups that had once been kings.

Early in the 21st century, the Internet Explorer's dominance was firmly entrenched, and by the third quarter of 2002, its *share stood at roughly 95%, more than Netscape ever had at its peak.* Since 2001, when IE 6.0 had been released, the first major upgrade was with the release of IE 7.0, in the fall of 2006, timed with the release of the Microsoft *Vista* operating system.

Fig. 7.3 shows the rise and fall of the Netscape browser and the accompanying rise of the Internet Explorer.

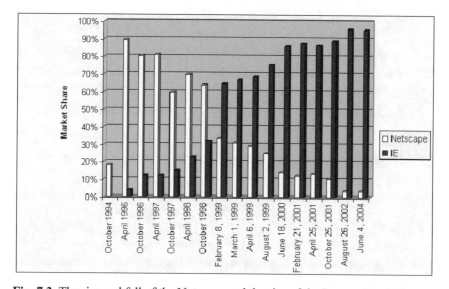

Fig. 7.3. The rise and fall of the Netscape and the rise of the Internet Explorer

---

Box 7.3: And like the Phoenix…

The battle for the browser market may not be over yet. In 1998, Netscape was sold to America Online which had been shopping around for some time for a browser. Earlier Netscape had released its source code under an open source license, calling the new product Mozilla (initially baptized Phoenix!) However it took almost four years for the first version, Mozilla1.0, to be released in 2002. A derivative product, the Firefox browser was released in 2004. It quickly became popular in the open source community. By the end of 2005, Internet Explorer´s share of the browser market had dropped to 85% (see also table 7.1).

Like the proverbial Phoenix, the Firefox symbolizes Netscape´s reincarnation. A small, but staunch (and growing) band of the open source community, spearheaded by the Linux operating system, started using the Firefox browser. Taking a leaf from the earlier Microsoft strategy, Firefox (and other open source software) often came bundled with Linux. Besides, the Internet Explorer was susceptible to viruses, adware and spyware. More resistant to these attacks, Firefox also didn't allow pop-ups. The browser wars in the earlier decade may not yet be over as Netscape and its later incarnation fight to stay alive.

(continued)

Box 7.3: And like the Phoenix… (cont.)

In October of 2006, both the Internet Explorer (IE 7.0) as well as that of Firefox (Firefox 4.0) came up with new versions. Firefox 4.0 incorporates spelling features. IE 7.0 is touted to have better security features, among other innovations.

7.5 Integrated Model and the Browser Story

The rather dramatic story of the rise and fall of an internet technology start up lends itself to interesting analyses using the Integrated Model. Figure 7.4 traces the browser wars in the integrated innovation space. We relied on subjective analyses of the respective browser capabilities to assess the browser positions in the archetype space (based on commentaries and opinion in technology blogs).

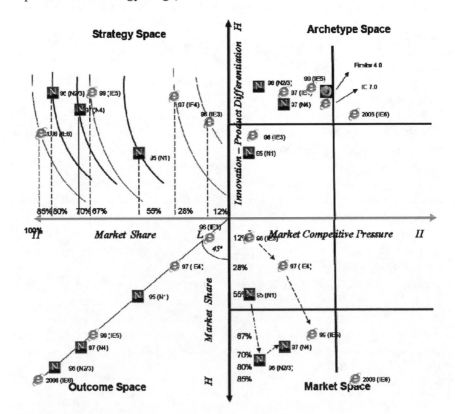

Fig. 7.4. Browser wars in the integrated innovation space

Table 7.1 below summarizes the browser market shares of Netscape and the Internet Explorer from 1995 onwards. Figures from the table were used to plot the respective market shares in the integrated innovation space of Fig. 7.4. The latest incarnations (IE 7.0 and Firefox 4.0) are considered by most analysts similarly positioned in terms of functionalities, which is reflected by their close positioning in the archetype space. The outcome space however does not reflect the relative market shares as too short a time has passed to give meaningful dynamics of this nature.

Table 7.1. Browser market shares

	Netscape	Internet Explorer	Mozilla Firefox
October 1996	80.45%	12.18%	-
January 1997	70%	28%	-
March, 1999	31.21%	66.90%	-
Q4 2004	2.09%	91.35%	3.66%
Q1 2005	1.89%	89.02%	6.17%
Q2 2005	1.62%	87.24%	8.08%
Q3 2005	1.92%	86.74%	7.97%
Q4 2005	1.25%	85.88%	9.00%
Q1 2006	1.09%	85.01%	9.77%
Q2 2006	0.98%	84.03%	10.67%
Q3 2006	0.88%	82.88%	11.89%

Source: Wikipedia

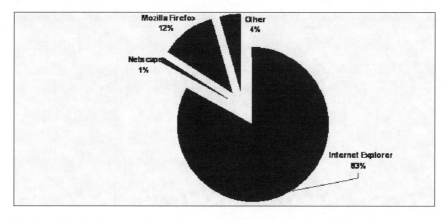

Fig. 7.5. Market Shares of web browsers (Q3 2006). Source: Wikipedia

Fig. 7.5 presents market share statistics of web browsers as of the third quarter of 2006 (Source: Wikipedia). Internet Explorer continues to hold sway, with about 83% of the market share, followed by Mozilla Firefox (about 12%). After the launch of latest versions, Internet Explorer is reported to have recovered some market share, reaching a share of around 85,9% (against 11,5% of Firefox)[20].

---

[20] http://www.windowsitpro.com/Windows/Article/ArticleID/93852/93852.html

8 Commoditization – The Sword of Damocles

And so, the next day, Damocles was led into the palace, and all the servants were
bidden to treat him as their master. ...
Then he chanced to raise his eyes toward the ceiling. What was it that was
dangling above him, with it's point almost touching his head? It was a sharp
sword, and it was hung by only a single horsehair. What if the hair should break?
There was danger every moment that it would do so.

...

"What is the matter?" said the tyrant.
"That sword! That sword!" cried Damocles. .."Yes," said Dionysius, "I know there
is a sword above your head, and that it may fall at any moment. But why should
that trouble you? I have a sword over my head all the time. I am every moment in
dread lest something may cause me to lose my life."

The Sword of Damocles, as retold by *James Baldwin*

8.1 Commoditization: The Call of the Sheep

In the previous two chapters we witnessed the constant efforts of firms to
stay at the top as witnessed in the case of the iPod, or to lead a fight back
by continuously innovating (LEGO, Barbie) and the rapid rise and dramatic fall of an erstwhile digital giant (Netscape). In each of the cases, the
Integrated Model provided a useful framework for analyses. Yet another
threat for firms is that of commoditization. Like the proverbial sword of
Damocles, there is a constant and impending threat of commoditization
looming over even the most innovative products. When price becomes the
lowest common denominator, managers increasingly scratch their heads,
wondering not of how to remain a wolf, but how to differentiate themselves and manage to stay in fox territory. *Commoditization is the gravity
pull of the sheep in the archetype space of the Integrated Model.*

In order to understand the threat of commoditization, it is important to
understand the dynamics of innovation, with a starting point being the understanding of a typical life cycle of a product. In Chap. 5, we had used the
Integrated Model to illustrate how innovative products can metamorphose

into fox and then finally end up in the low margin, non differentiating sheep territory. In this chapter we begin with an understanding of both the life cycle of a product as well as the technology life cycle (Sect. 8.2). The emergence of a dominant industrial design is discussed to better understand the commoditization process. Finally we explain commoditization in the integrated innovation space.

8.2 Commoditization, Product and the Technology Life Cycle

8.2.1 The Product Life Cycle

The product life cycle is a useful tool for understanding the stages through which a product typically passes, starting from its market introduction to maturity to eventual withdrawal. Based on the metaphor of a biological life cycle, like the plantation of a seed, a product is first introduced into the market, after which it sees its acceptance and growth (sprouting of the seed). The product then arrives to a maturity phase then slips into gradual decline and witnesses an eventual withdrawal from the market (death of the plant). Fig. 8.1 below illustrates these five stages of a typical product life cycle.

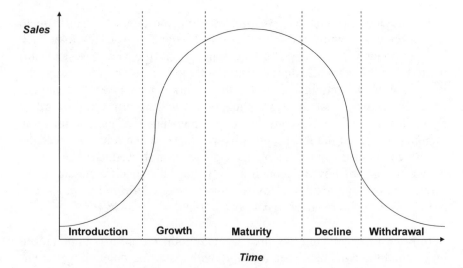

Fig. 8.1. The product life cycle

In terms of per unit production costs, a corresponding unit cost curve would display a downward sloping trend (curve not shown), with costs declining as the product progresses along the product life cycle trajectory. The increased sales volume associated with the maturity stage quickly leads a product towards the *commodity* phase where the specialized characteristics of the product are less prominent, unit production costs are low and rival competitors have already emerged.

8.2.2 The Technology Life Cycle and Dominant Design

Technology plays an increasingly important role not just in determining the time frame of the product life cycle. The way technology evolves over the life cycle of a product can be crucial in understanding the commoditization process. A good starting point for understanding the linkages between technology and the product life cycle is the technology adoption S-curve which traces out the evolution of the performance of a technology over time.

Richard Foster[1] describes the typical progression of technology as follows. During the nascent stage of a new technology, R&D has a significant weight along with other resources, but only small performance improvements are observed. However this soon changes with the accumulation of more knowledge and an increase in the adoption of the technology leads to enhanced performance. Soon performance improves at an exponential rate with small expenditures on research resulting in powerful innovation (performance) gains. However this passes a certain inflexion point, after which the performance productivity of investment declines, soon approaching a physical limit. Fig 8.2 plots a typical *technology S-curve*. Note that if in the vertical axis, we substituted product sales performance as the variable, and then the curve described would be the adoption curve of Rogers (see Box 1.4). Recall that Everett Rogers described the process of the spread of innovation through society, with the S-curve as the cumulative adoption curve.

---

[1] See Foster (1986), chap. 4.

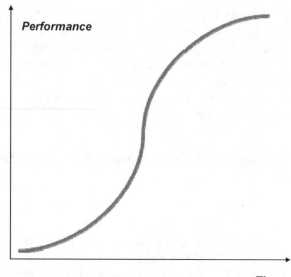

Fig. 8.2. The technology S-curve

Box 8.1: A mouse along the S-curve

An interesting example of the adoption of technology (embodied in a product) and performance limits is that of the computer mouse. Invented in 1932 by Douglas Engelbert, it was only in the late nineteen eighties that its adoption became widespread. Englbert felt that there was a need for a pointing device that would allow more efficient interaction between the user and the graphical user interface (GUI) thus the mouse was originally designed to help increase labour productivity.

Patented on 1970, the first mouse used two perpendicular wheels and just one button. In the early 1970's the first ball mouse was invented that enabled rotations in all directions. With the passage of time, mice improved in performance and augmented capacities, with decrease in size. Nowadays it is possible to use wireless optical mice, with scroll wheels, with two buttons (since middle 1990's) or even three. There are also mice for computer games, which are more precise and quick and Laptops with mice incorporated. As the usage of computer mice increased, the computer mouse industry has also slowly diffused into other industries.

In their study on the diffusion of innovation, Abernathy and Utterback[2] take the S-curve further. In their influential analysis of the dynamics of innovation, the authors explain the emergence of a dominant design by studying the different phases in the technology life cycle.

In the early days of a new technology there exists enormous potential for its application. No-one knows quite what to do with it. This early phase is characterized by lots of experimentation and there exist many variations of the product or service around the technology and its applications. The market is fluid with people taking risks since the stakes are low. Consumers for this product like novelty. Uncertainty faces both producers and these consumers in this stage.

In these early stages, there is no standard. But gradually these experiments begin to converge around a *dominant design*. This dominant standard is often best from both a technical and user perspective, and it is this standard that set up the rules of the game.

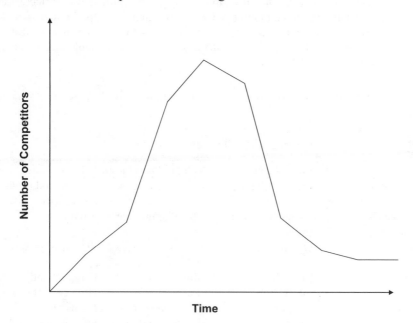

Fig. 8.3. The emergence of a dominant design

---

[2] See Abernathy and Clark (1978).

Once the dominant design emerges, either of products or processes; the focus moves from experimentation to refining the dominant design. At this stage, only a small number of firms survive the transition from the earlier fluid phase. As the technology matures even further, this incremental innovation becomes more significant and the focus shifts to cost reductions and efficiency improvements, on scale economies and on process innovation. The process innovation leads to large scale specialized production units.

As the market matures even further, it is then that the commoditization phase sets in according to Abernathy and Utterback.

> "As the market matures the product or service is "commoditized". This term denotes a competitive environment in which product differentiation is difficult, customer loyalty and brand values are low, competition is based primarily on price, and sustainable advantage comes from cost leadership. Commoditization is driven by excess capacity. There are recurring cycles in investment, capacity utilization, prices, and profitability. In commoditized markets intense competition de-couples prices from costs, margins are highly sensitive to capacity utilization, innovation slows or stops and the sources of sustainable advantage are less tangible."

The table below sets out the characteristics of each of these stages in life cycle.

Table 8.1. Stages in the innovation life cycle

	Fluid Phase	Transitional Phase	Specific Phase
Innovation	Product changes	Process changes	Incremental product and process
Source of innovation	New entrants or users	Manufacturers or users	Suppliers
Products	Diverse design	At least one with stable features	Standard products
Production	Flexible and inefficient	More rigid	Efficient and rigid. High cost of change
R&D	Unspecified focus. High uncertainty	Focus on specific product features	Focus on incremental product technologies and process technology.
Competitors	Few but with growing market shares	Many but declining numbers	Few, oligopoly with stable market shares

Table 8.1. Stages in the innovation life cycle (cont.)

	Fluid Phase	Transitional Phase	Specific Phase
Competitors	Few but with growing market shares	Many but declining numbers	Few, oligopoly with stable market shares
Basis of competition	Functional product performance	Product variation and *fitness for use*	Price
Organizational control	Informal and entrepreneurial	Project and task groups	Structure, rules and goals
Vulnerabilities	To imitators and patent challenges	To more efficient and higher-quality producers	To superior product substitutes

Adapted from: www.innovation.lth.se/files/Undergraduate/Mastering_the_Dynamics_of_Innovation.pdf

8.2.3 Commoditization, Functionality and Modularization

Clayton Christensen[3] whose insight into disruptive technologies we had seen earlier in Chaps. 2 and 5 provides an interesting framework for the new product lifecycle. His thesis traces out the lifecycle of a product on the *basis on which a product is competing.* According to one technology blog[4]:

> "Early in the product lifecycle firms differentiate their products based on functionality. Given that the production requires deep technical knowledge there is a single provider integrating product parts. Firms are able to achieve proprietary margins for their expertise, given that this knowledge is not widely available. As the product category matures, the basis of competition becomes product reliability, then to convenience and finally to price. Commoditization stage is reached when price becomes the basis of competition."

Thus according to Christensen, in the early stages of the product life cycle, the owner of proprietary architecture earns attractive profit margins. First because differentiation is relatively easy and second because of the high ratio of fixed to variable costs. However trying to keep ahead of its competitors, according to Christensen, leads to an overshooting when the product provides more functionality and reliability than demanded by lesser demanding customers (thus laying the grounds for *disruptive*

---

[3] See Christensen and Raynor (2003).
[4] www.venchar.com/2003/09/standards_and_c.html

innovation to occur). This precipitates a change in the basis of competition towards the product becoming *modular and conformable*[5].

This evolution toward modular architectures facilitates the disintegration of the industry making it difficult for the product to differentiate itself from its competitors either on performance or cost. This is because the competitors have access to the same components and assemble according to the same standards. In this modularization stage much less expertise is required to build the product. Christensen gives the example of the personal computer to illustrate this process. When first constructed by IBM, constructing a PC required a lot of expertise to integrate the different components. But as, the components became more powerful and the integration mechanism (motherboard) became commoditized, margins fell. The commoditization phase had set in. Component and motherboard manufacturers make tiny margins.

Thus according to Christensen[6]:

> "A product becomes a commodity within a specific market segment when the repeated changes in the basis of competition completely play themselves out, i.e., when market needs on each attribute or dimension of performance have been fully satisfied by more than one available product."

The authors believe that simultaneous to the commoditization process there is a decommoditization at work at someplace else in the value chain, which affords opportunities for differentiating and capturing high margins.

Earlier in Chap. 5, in Sect. 5.3, we described how the entire product life cycle is getting squeezed into the time that it once took just to get the product into the market. Products ranging from consumer goods to high technology information goods are hurtling on the way to commoditization. The Integrated Model illustrated the product life cycle as a metamorphoses of a product from wolf to fox and finally sheep.

The Integrated Model can further illustrate the commoditization process as described by Christensen and Raynor. Fig. 8.4 combines the decommoditization idea in the product life cycle in the integrated innovation space.

---

[5] See Box 2.3 on *disruptive innovation*.
[6] See Christensen (1997), p. 217.

Box 8.2: Commoditization as a strategy

While commoditization can be the low cost producer's trump card, can it actually be a strategy move by dominant firms such as Intel. Economists term such pricing practice as predatory pricing, whereby a product is sold at a very low price with the intent of driving competitors out of the industry. The low price charged by the incumbent firm can act as an entry barrier for a potential entrant to the industry.

Intel's pricing strategy was noted by the Harvard Business School Professor, Nicholas Carr (see the *Wired Magazine*, May 2004, available at www.wired.com/wired/archive/12.05/view.html?pg=2).

"According to *The Wall Street Journal*, Intel is selling its Centrino Wi-Fi chips for at the its fabrication cost. Why? For one thing, turning Wi-Fi technology into a cheap commodity may be a good way to defeat compeition. More important, making Wi-Fi chips broadly affordable encourages people to buy laptops, and selling laptop chipsets is far more lucrative for Intel than selling desktop chipsets. It's in Intel's interest to commoditize Wi-Fi as quickly as possible.

The author also notes that the commoditization strategy of technology giants is not confined to just Intel. Other firms such Sun Microsystems, in promoting the open source office suite software package of StarOffice, hopes to provide a viable alternative to Microsoft Office, as a way to break into Microsoft´s desktop dominance. IBM is on a similar track of trying to usurp Microsoft´s throne in its vigorous promotion Linux, for PCs and servers. Microsoft in turn can be accused of pursuing a selective commoditization strategy by giving away the Internet Explorer, or by bundling its Windows Media Player with its operating system. Selective commoditization is pursued by all these giants as an effort to unseat big market players in particular areas. Google's strategy of offering its host of free online softwares, from mapping to word processing can also be seen as an attempt to make inroads into others turf.

8.3 Standardization, Commoditization and the China Price

Standardization can play an important role in speeding up the product lifecycle by tending to remove competition based on features and functionality. This is true not only in traditional manufactures but increasingly in the technology industry. For instance as one technology blog notes, most of the core functionality of a product category such as

WiFi AP is now standardized and it is very hard for access point (AP) manufacturers to differentiate their offerings[7]. The emergence of a standard has also other impacts: (1) it signals a broad consensus on specifications, (2) it encourages multi-vendor adoption of the standard, (3) competition between vendors drives down the cost, (4) lower costs drive adoption, which leads to even lower costs in a vicious/virtuous cycle. In the past, the computer PC manufacturing industry has gone through exactly this cycle. This is also true for the entire computer industry in general. As noted in an influential article published in 2000, by the economist Robert Gordon[8]:

> "A second distinguishing feature of the development of the computer industry, after the decline in price, is the unprecedented speed with which diminishing returns set in."

In a global context, one side effect of standardization is to encourage and ease the entry of low cost manufacturers, especially of original design manufacturers (ODM) from China and Taiwan. These ODMs are able to thrive due to their low-cost products and higher volumes and also due to the standardization brought in by the openness of specifications and multi-vendor support for components.

Today we are witnessing commoditization even in high value added services like design. According to some experts all the intellectual property today increasingly resides in the chip. To quote for instance the CEO of Flextronics, one of the largest ODM companies (that partner with large companies like Dell, HP, Motorola, Microsoft and other big name companies in designing and manufacturing their products).

> "You can make a cell phone on a chip. You can make a router on a chip. Pretty soon you'll have cellular base stations on a chip. *Every product is on a trajectory of becoming silicon surrounded by plastic.*"

---

[7] www.venchar.com, Sep. 3, 2003.
[8] See Gordon (2000).

Box 8.3: The China Price

In December of 2004, the Business Week magazine ran a cover on China entitled "The China Price". A phrase which has come to mean the low rate at which a good or service can be provided by China. The weekly narrated the major impact that Chinese imports were having on US businesses. The emergence of Chinese manufacturing might was not just being felt in consumer goods manufactures, but also further up the technology value chain, including networking gear and chip manufacturing. The article noted the erosion of American manufacturing vis a vis China and saw a future where China would also be an innovating giant. Business Week thus noted on the Chinese focus on innovation:

"And Chinese producers are hardly standing still. In a recent survey of Chinese and U.S. manufacturers by IndustryWeek and Cleveland-based Manufacturing Performance Institute, 54% of Chinese companies cited innovation as one of their top objectives, while only 26% of U.S. respondents did. Chinese companies spend more on worker training and enterprise-management software. And 91% of U.S. plants are more than a decade old, vs. 54% in China."

While cheap imports, especially of consumer goods ranging from toys to electronics, spell fear to manufacturers all over the world, for the western consumer there has been unprecedented real price decline. Discount stores such as Wal-Mart have benefited enormously from Chinese manufactures, a benefit that has been passed on to the consumers. Nearly 10% of all Chinese exports to the United States are accounted from by Wal-Mart alone. Author Oded Shenkar speaks of the wider implications of the surge of Chinese exports (see Shenkar (2004)).

"The commoditization of previously branded products has brought into the market consumers who in the past could not afford the product and enabled others to shift portions of their disposable income toward the purchase of higher level or a broader array of products and services, including those domestically made. At the same time, the flood of Chinese imports is creating unprecedented pressures on manufacturers who rely on brand name or country-of-origin impact (such as Italian leather goods), especially for below-luxury products, which were already pressured by the expansion of large discounters."

8.4 Commoditization: The Wolf in Sheep's Clothing

The Integrated Model can provide us with valuable insights into the commoditization process, from the birth of a wolf to its ultimate (and increasingly rapid) metamorphosis into sheep. In Chap. 5 we had illustrated the general nature of this metamorphosis. In this section, the Integrated Model illustrates some key developments in the commoditization path. While we (as do most other authors) use the information technology industry to exemplify commoditization, the process described by the Integrated Model is illustrative of other industries as well, including automobiles.

In a 2003 article[9], published by the Harvard Business Review (later to be followed by a book on the same theme), that drew torrents of debate especially from the industry; Nicholas Carr argued that IT cannot be relied upon to provide a competitive edge to firms. He held that IT has become a commodity just like a utility, and rivals quickly eliminate any gains from its application by adopting the same or similar technology. The ubiquity of information technology essential for business process no longer translates into a differentiating factor for firms. While ownership and adoption of technology in the early stages bestows advantages to a firm, this window is open only briefly. IT according to Carr has all the hallmarks of an infrastructural technology.

Carr makes a distinction between proprietary technology and infrastructural technology. Proprietary technology such as patents, specific knowledge or innovation, exclusive rights to a new technology etc., is owned by the firm, and affords protection to the firm. This enables the firm to reap higher profits than rivals. Infrastructural technology such as railroads, telegraphs, power generators, broadband etc., become part of the general business infrastructure. The signs of commoditization having set in are visible according to Carr in many ways.

> "First IT's power is outstripping most of the business needs it fulfils. Second, the price of essential IT functionality has dropped to the point where it is more or less affordable to all. Third the capacity of universal distribution network (the Internet) has caught up with demand-indeed, we have considerably more fiber-optic capacity than we need. Fourth, IT vendors are rushing to position themselves as commodity suppliers or even as utilities. Finally, and most definitively, the investment bubble has

---

[9] See Carr (2003).

burst, which historically has been a clear indication that an information technology is reaching its buildout."

Let us relate the story of a wolf. Owner of proprietary technology, for many years she enjoyed high profits. Much like computer manufacturers such as IBM in it's hey days as the mainframe computer industry king or DEC or Data General, the wolf had proprietary products, distinct cost advantages and high entry barriers. Like IBM that delivered an end-to-end solution to the customer, from the hardware on up through the operating system her customers were locked in to the wolf.

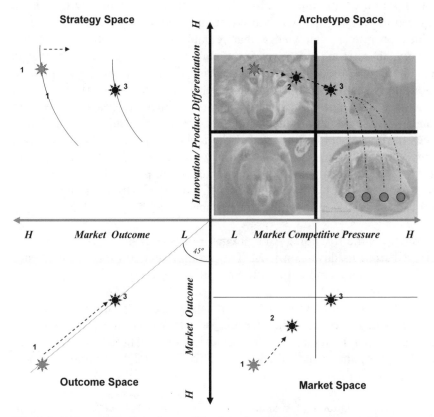

Fig. 8.4. Commoditization: the wolf in sheep's clothing

The integrated and proprietary nature of the industry implied that the wolf enjoyed substantial market dominance. Fig. 8.4 above illustrates the wolf (position 1 in the figure) in the integrated innovation space.

However a string of factors gradually loosened the wolf's stranglehold on the market. Other firms seized the opportunity to move into the market opened up by the wolf, a market dominated by consumers who were satisfied by 'good enough' quality at a lower price. Much like firms such as Apple, Apollo and Sun that saw an open window of opportunity to cater to a new tier of the computing consumer—the individual user.

The wolf's shift to fox territory starts assuming its own dynamic as the industry moves towards modularity and disintegration. As we discussed before, the evolution toward modular architectures, facilitates the disintegration of the industry. Standardization sets in, whereby the inputs required in building the wolf's product can be bought off the shelf. There is little proprietary knowledge that remains with the wolf. Now in fox territory, there is an accompanying metamorphosis of the product that is being sold. The modularity and splintering of the manufacturing process could imply that the firm is now merely an assembler of the product, and sometimes even not that. The proprietary architecture has given way to standardized, modular products, coming from different suppliers inhabiting sheep territory. This is illustrated in the archetype space in Fig. 8.4. Rival firms with access to similar technology (remember IT as a utility) and access to the same suppliers of the standardized inputs, substantially erode the profits enjoyed by the erstwhile wolf. This is illustrated in the shifting to the left of the IP curve in the strategy space (Fig. 8.4) from 1 to 3.

So who is the fox now? An aggregator of parts. Often a brand that has survived from its days as a wolf. The strong brand still enables it to earn profits, albeit much more difficult than before.

The only way for the wolf to regain its erstwhile position, albeit in a market more competitive than before, is to focus on other aspects of the value chain that it can tap into to provide profits. As noted by Christensen and Raynor[10], the locus of erstwhile powerful brands migrates to new locations:

> "The migration of branding power in a market that is composed of multiple tiers is a process, not an event. Accordingly, the brands of companies with proprietary products typically create value mapping from their position on the improvement trajectory-toward those customers who are still not satisfied with the functionality and reliability of the best that is available. But mapping downward from that same point-toward the

---

[10] Christensen and Raynor (2003), pp. 163-164.

world of modular products where speed, convenience, and responsiveness drive competitive success-the power to create profitable brands migrates away from the end-use product, toward the subsystems and the channel."

The change in the basis of competition can often result in a change in the way the firm does business itself, or even the very business. Innovation for the wolf can be in the supply chain, protecting the brand, providing a unique customer experience or anything that enables it to differentiate itself and provide value to the consumer in a world that is witnessing a disintegration of production.

9 Escape from Commoditization?

When one door closes another door opens;
but we so often look so long and so regretfully upon the closed door,
that we do not see the ones which open for us.

Alexander Graham Bell

9.1 Any Escape from Commoditization?

The commoditization trap seems to be the inescapable destiny of products, even as firms continuously try to differentiate their products in their attempts at standing out. Sometimes better design seems to be one of the few escape routes available, albeit temporary, in slowing the slide towards the end of the product life cycle. Breakthrough innovations hold the only real key to escaping from commoditization.

Which brings us to the interesting question - how is it that firms whose products could be considered almost *homogenous*[1] from the economists point of view, are able to stay alive, indeed often thrive? Not only do many products have fundamental characteristics that are intrinsically similar across the sector, but are somehow able to not only differentiate but also elude the commoditization trap.

In this chapter we focus on one such case of an apparent escape from the commoditization trap, that of search engines. Although a careful analysis of the business of search engines is beyond the scope of this chapter, the attempts at differentiation by search engines (with the integrated innovation space forming the framework) hold interesting insights into the strategies employed in differentiation.

---

[1] In economics, a homogenous product is considered to be a "product of an industry in which the outputs of different firms are indistinguishable", as explained by Professor Deardoff of the University of Michigan. (see in www-personal.umich.edu/~alandear/glossary/h.html#pagetop

9.2 Search as God

Time was when search engines were add-on services for portals. Firms like Yahoo and America Online (AOL) incorporated search services to their portals for their users who could trawl through web pages in search of information when needed. This quickly changed starting from the late 1990s, motivated by three factors. First due to an explosion of the internet in terms of the number of web pages and information therein. The internet which had started which had 19000 websites in 1995, was populated in November 2006 with something around 101,4 million websites, according to Netcraft[2]. Navigating once way through this immense maze of information could only be meaningfully done by search engines.

The second factor accounting for the rise of search engines was a corresponding boom in the number of internet users. Not surprisingly the United States leads the world with a penetration rate of almost 70% of the population using the internet. Overall, the growth rate of internet use has been a staggering 183% annually over the six year period from 2000 to 2005. In some parts of the world, like in the Middle East and Africa, the growth rate has been more than twice this, albeit from a much smaller base. In the United States alone the average growth has been over 118% annually[3].

These two factors combined to create the third factor- the web as a place which was a must for firm online presence. Firms like *eBay* and *Amazon* demonstrated how the internet could be the medium to undertake successful business (see Box 9.3 to get a measure of the financial clout of these firms). Ever more people were not only logging on to the net, but were spending increasing amounts of time there - using e-mail, shopping, socializing or just surfing. As we can see from Fig. 9.1 below the average user in the United States now spends about 1 hour time daily on the internet (as reported by Nielsen).

With the virtual world of the World Wide Web playing an ever increasing role in people's lives, search engines began to start acquiring lives of their own, apart from the portals that used to carry them. However it was

---

[2]http://news.netcraft.com/archives/2006/09/index.html;
  http://survey.netcraft.com/Reports/9508/ALL/
[3] Source: Internet World Statistics.

with the founding of *Google* by two Stanford PhD Stanford[4] Sergey Brin, and Larry Page in the late 1990s (see Box 9.3 for a brief story on Google) not only did search engines find their place in the digital sun, but they also showed how they could actually be good business. The astronomical rise of Google, both as a search engine as well as a revenue generator reflected in its share price and its stratospheric market valuations (see Box 9.3).

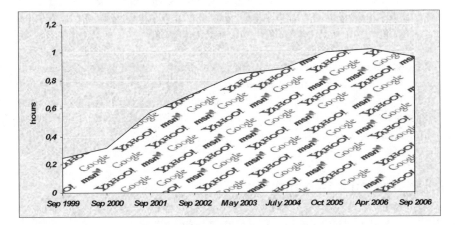

Fig. 9.1. Are you online? Daily time spent (in hours) on the internet.
Source: Nielsen

Even before Google's spectacular burst into Wall Street with its IPO in August 2004, people were beginning to realize the importance of search engines. The *New York Times* columnist and author of a popular book on outsourcing and globalization[5], Thomas Friedman, wrote a column in 2003, asking: "Is Google God?" Realization had begun to sink in of the search engine's importance in an increasingly internet driven lifestyle.

Search engines have become an increasingly important part of the online experience of American internet users. A survey of online consumer behaviour by the Pew Internet & American showed that about 60 million American adults are using search engines on a typical day. Search was only second to e-mail (74 million users per day, in September 2005) as the most popular activity on the internet[6].

---

[4] For two fascinating accounts on the birth and the rise of Google, see Battelle (2005) and Vise and Malseed (2005).

[5] See Friedman (2005).

[6] http://www.pewinternet.org/PPF/r/167/report_display.asp

Firms discovered that internaut eyeballs were worth paying for, and search engines emerged as a profitable area based on advertising revenue. One report by *eMarketer* estimated that Google is expected to grab 57% of the approximately $16 billion spent on paid search advertising in the U.S. in 2006. Yahoo, the next biggest competitor, is expected to nab 27% of this pie. Advertisers also found the internet finally a medium where their advertising dollars are based on actual viewership, with the pay per click advertising model. Indeed the move towards pay per buy in online advertising is the ultimate dream of advertising mangers.

Besides paying to advertise in order to snare search traffic, enterprise search solutions (ESS) are also an added revenue generator with Google launching its ESS in February of 2002. Organizations from Boeing to Sony Ericsson to the World Bank[7] are using such solutions to find information within their organizational intranet.

9.3 Is Search a Commodity?

With so much riding on internet search, both for users as well as businesses, it begets the question - is search a commodity? With zero switching costs, users can opt for whichever search engine that takes their fancy at any given time. Hence in principle at least, ignoring habits or brand name association, the more efficient and accurate a search engine, the more user base it would have. This strategy therefore implies ever more investment in technology and innovation coupled with making the interface more user friendly. To a large extent this has precisely been the strategy followed by Google, coupled with an ever expanding array of free services, most but not all based on search. Its closest competitor Yahoo too is vigorously pursuing a user loyalty strategy.

Google's power to capture both attention as well as share holder confidence (hopes?) can be attributed to many things. First was its timing. Its arrival in the late 1990s coincided exactly the time of the Web explosion and a consequent user need to find their way through the html jungle. The second reason was a conscious differentiation strategy based on focus, heavy artillery and an every more array of complementary services. Google regularly hires some of the best brains and talent in the business (with even a lawsuit in 2005 by Microsoft alleging poaching of one of its

---

[7] List of customers can be found on the Google website.

top executives). With a large number of PhDs in its ranks (and no separate research division) Google has a total workforce of almost 9400 people[8], many of whom are engineers. Goggle engineers stay focus on doing one thing only, search. To promote a culture of innovation, development staff are reportedly allowed one day a week to work on their own projects, becoming a model for other technology companies on promoting innovation. Google products such as the *gmail*, *Google News* and the internet socializing site *Orkut*, are reported to have been born from personal projects of some of Google's employees.

Google tries to maintain brand loyalty by strenuously separating of (and being seen so) *religion from politics*. Thus the commercial side of advertisements is kept discretely on the side of search results. Users remain loyal because they feel their searches have been 'unadulterated' by commercial interests. Indeed Google's motto is *"do no evil"* and its web site ranks the ten corporate commandments. Of course with the goal being to create the *perfect* search engine.

For accuracy and efficiency, Google maintains immense hardware artillery that constantly trolls through billions of websites caching for information. However it is not just hardware that has assured Google supremacy, its technology and innovation. For instance the page rank algorithm that it uses for its searches ensures the most efficient way to get search results. It assigns a *PageRank*, to every web page, which is a function of the number of page links to and from another page. This was an innovation in web search by creating a page reputation.

And thus was created a differentiation strategy, a brand name for Google, synonymous with effective search. With *"googling"* now a verb for search, user loyalty checks any slide into commoditization, even with other powerful engines hovering in the digital space.

Yahoo Search, the firm Google upstaged, on the other hand was born a portal, and continues to be one, with an apparently different corporate philosophy. As a former manager at Yahoo noted[9]:

> "Yahoo is investing in differentiating services rather than competing head on with Google...The classic difference between Yahoo and Google...is

---

[8] September 30, 2006.

[9] John Zapolski was the former creative director at Yahoo! This quote appeared in The Business Week, May 17, 2006.

that Yahoo is more about people. Google is more on algorithms and powerful engineering."

Yahoo's differentiation strategy has therefore been personalization and promotion of virtual communities. Yahoo is increasingly a *one stop shop* for its users, offering everything from news to weather and creation of directories for everything from travel to shopping. It positions itself as *more* than a search engine, which has resulted in Yahoo many more unique visitors than Google. According to Nielsen/NetRatings Google have a clear dominance in search. In October 2006 they accounted for around 50% of all searches, compared to 23,9% on Yahoo.

Box 9.1: A (very) brief history of search engines

The first tool used for searching on the Internet was "Archie", was created by a Canadian student in 1990. Archie downloaded the directory listings of all the files located on public anonymous FTP (File Transfer Protocol) sites, creating a searchable database of filenames. This was followed in 1991 with the creation of Gopher, which indexed text documents unlike Archie which indexed computer files. This was later followed by "Veronica" and "Jughead," (a play on the comic book series, following Archie, which however was named after Archive) which searched files stored in Gopher index systems

In 1993, from MIT was born the first Web search engine, a robot the World Wide Web Wanderer. While Archie and Veronica were manually indexed, the wanderer tracked the growth of the Web by counting web servers initially but quickly got URLs as well created the very first database of websites, called the Wandex.

1994 saw the birth of two "full text" web crawler-based search engines, the WebCrawler, and Lycos (from Carnegie Mellon University). Lycos became a major commercial endeavour, backed by a $2 million venture capital.

Later years were to see a host of other search engines like Excite, Infoseek, Inktomi, Ask Jeeves, and AltaVista. Most of them were more than search engines and competed with popular directories such as Yahoo!Yahoo! founded by two Stanford University students (much like Google) in 1995, started off as a listing of their favourite web sites.

(continued)

Box 9. 1: A (very) brief history of search engines (cont.)

In 2002, Yahoo! acquired Inktomi and in 2003, Overture, (which owned AlltheWeb and AltaVista).Despite owning its own search engine, Yahoo initially used Google to provide its users with search results on its main web site Yahoo.com. However since 2004, it developed and used its own search engine based on the combined technologies of its acquisitions.

Source: Wikipedia

In an attempt to create user fidelity, Yahoo's My Search 2.0 – uses personalization of embedded proprietary data in its searches. This feature tags pages of interest to the user and then restricts future searches to the tagged set. Keeping with the overall strategy of promoting virtual communities, the user can also ask friends to tag their frequently used pages, thereby focusing searches on *community pages*. This then makes switching costs harder for users, since the tagged data cannot be transferred to other search engines like Google.

However innovation by search engines appears to be a 'me too' strategy, with both Yahoo and Google learning from each other. Google, while maintaining its focus of being a search engine, has rapidly expanded the services associated with search such as customized news, book search, blog and video searches. Google desktop searches have proved to be an instant hit with users overtaking Microsoft Windows own desktop search engine (Windows Desktop Search) (Microsoft however countered with the release of the 3.0 version in October 2006). Google has gone to non search territory by providing digitalized version of books, Google Maps (a popular tool for many American users), chat, e-mail, VoIP etc. Indeed Google Labs is constantly churning out ever more 'beta' products and Google is gradually creeping into applications currently dominated by Microsoft. In October 2006 with the launch of its own spreadsheet and office application software (Google Docs & Spreadsheets), Google has made clear its intention of entering non search terrain.

Yahoo on the other hand has tried to give a boost to its muscle power (having long used Google's search engine) by first acquiring Inktomi in 2003 and later launching in 2004, its own search engine based on the combined technologies of its acquisitions. Google tried to follow Yahoo's success in virtual communities with Orkut, but so far with limited success, Brazil appearing to be the country with most users of Orkut.

Be what may, despite the constant attempts at creating user loyalty, low switching costs would implies an omnipresent threat of commoditization, like the sword of Damocles. For most people, search results are often very similar be it Google, Yahoo, MSN, AskJeeves etc., although there is some research that disputes this.

Thus the strategy that each search engine has employed is to try to increase switching costs. A complaint filed in 2006 by Google regarding Microsoft's sticking an embedded MSN toolbar in the Windows operating system, demonstrates the effort to increase 'stickiness' (by MSN) of its own users to a search engine, and Google's reaction as an indicator of the possible effectiveness of the strategy. But even that may be tenuous, since (and as Microsoft argued) a user can simply take off the option of putting MSN's search bar on the screen. Indeed all search engines, and for that matter ˊmyriad other technologies from web browsers to audio players, repeatedly attempt to make their program a default on the user's computer!

9.4 Innovation and Market Outcomes in the Case of Search Engines

The history of search engines, despite the surprising paucity of reliable data (see Box 9.2. relating to measurement issues), lends itself to fascinating analyses when applied to the Integrated Model. While so far we have eschewed from using two variables in the outcome space to keep our analyses tractable, the explosion of web search is a tempting invitation to study some dynamic analyses in the outcome space.

Using some of our own estimates as well as data from third party providers, we plotted the percentage share of searches against another outcome variable- the number of searches conducted. As web usage grew, the number of searches grew as well, search share remaining constant. Thus the exponential growth in the number of web pages is incorporated in the model as a parameter change in the integrated innovation space. This change is represented in the outcome space, for different time periods, as a swivelling of the curve outwards to the vertical axis (the function relating percentage search to number of searches).

Fig. 9.2 below describes the dynamics of innovation and market outcomes using the Integrated Model, for the case of the two largest search engines Yahoo Search and Google.

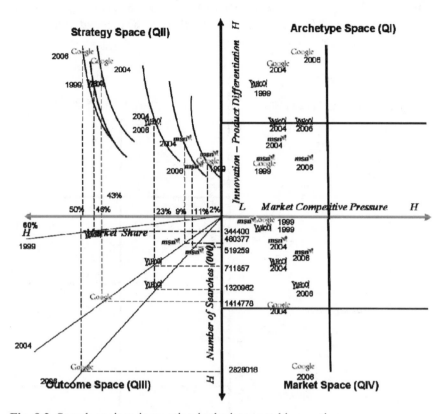

Fig. 9.2. Search engines-innovation in the integrated innovation space

In the integrated innovation space, we trace the relative positions of MSN, Yahoo Search and Google, starting from 1999. The relative positions in the archetype space are suggestive, drawn mostly from technology and user reports.

In the outcome space, we opted to include two distinct dimensions - market share (share of search engine usage) and the number of searches. These two variables are shown related in a given time period by a ray at a given angle from the origin. However, this ray (that relates search share to number of searches), swivels over time, with the angle increasing as the number of users increases. We show three such cases for the years 1999, 2004 and 2006.

In Fig. 9.3 in the following page we illustrate the relative positions in the integrated space for the year 2006. AOL is also included. The search share data is the same as shown in Fig. 9.4.

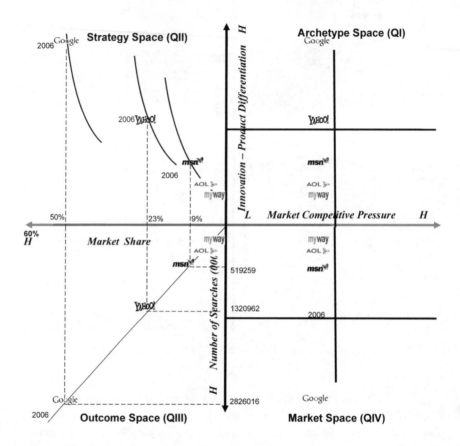

Fig. 9.3. Search engines: position in September 2006

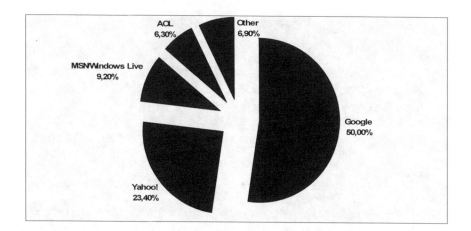

Fig. 9.4. Relative positions in the integrated space for the year 2006

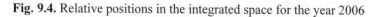

Box 9.2: Search engine statistics

In our outcome space, the two outcome variables we chose were –the share of total searches (market share indicator) and the total number of searches. While the share statistic was relatively easy to find after the year 2000, we had to do use some own estimates and extrapolation for total searches executed. While search engine firms like Yahoo search, Google and Ask have their own traffic data, this is confidential information. Third–party companies such as Nielsen/NetRatings and Jupiter Media Metrix sell data of search shares and audience reach, defined by the number of unique visitors to a search engine in a given time span. Given the enormous implications of being highly ranked in searches, consultancies and market intelligence companies have sprung up.

Statistics of the third party companies we discovered are often not comparable, and more so before the year 2000 (indeed we suspect that only towards the end of the previous century were data collection of searches taken seriously. Prior to the focus appeared to be in getting unique audience data, which could be for portals or search engines. The reports vary in the coverage area, with some focusing on home audience, others on work as well. Some have US data, others have global data.

(continued)

Box 9.2: Search engine statistics (cont.)

Besides the data has to be read with some caution, as noted by one site, *firstmonday*, (http://www.firstmonday.org/), about the confusion in the difference in how popularity (the variable we use for market result) is interpreted. As noted by the source:

> "Popularity can mean, at the most basic level, two very distinct things:
> a) percentage of users who turn to a search engine for their search needs;

and

> b) percentage of all search queries that are run on a particular search engine
>
> ... The two measures are not interchangeable. It is highly likely that some users account for a disproportionately large number of all search queries performed on the Web. Users who spend more time online and who turn to search engines more during their Web use are likely to account for much more of search engine traffic than users who spend less time on the Web or who do not use search engines often. If we are interested in the number of distinct individuals who are exposed to a search engine, then the former measure will be more informative. If we want to know which search engines process the most queries regardless of who is doing the searching, then the latter statistic will contain the answer."

It is also useful to remember that Google search engine power other search engine sites as well. These search sites obtain their results from Google's search engine in response to their queries and add their own content before listing Google's results.

Clearly Google's strategy has been one of differentiating from others using strong artillery as well as coming up with other products to snare traffic, in at attempt to harvest site traffic to generate advertising revenue. The acquisition of *YouTube*, the popular video sharing site, in fall of 2006, marks one more step in this direction, trying to create *stickiness*. Paradoxically while search engines send users elsewhere, the myriad add on services that Google already provides from social networking to mapping to video sharing, are all about strategizing for surfers to comeback! As noted by John Delaney of the Ovum. Consumer Group:

> "If something comes along which offers a better search experience, people can switch at once. There's no stickiness to search. The reason YouTube works better is because it has a community element which makes it harder for people as individuals to find the same thing elsewhere.[10]"

---

[10] http://business.guardian.co.uk/story/0,,1892325,00.html

Box 9.3: Do you Google?

Google is a play on the word *googol*, coined by the American mathematician Milton Sirotta to represents the number 1 followed by 100 zeroes. The choice of this as the company name by the two Stanford PhD students who founded the company in September 7, 1998, reflected the immense amount of information available on the web. The two fascinating books by Battelle (2005) and Vise and Malseed (2005) describe the creation of the company and its subsequent meteoric rise. Google made the unfashionable and drab internet search into a sexy, profitable company, and so far has been rewarded extremely handsomely in the stock market. Its total market capitalization at $149 billion is far superior to many large giants, indeed greater than many taken together like Walt Disney, GM and Ford, as we can see from the table below.

Table Box 9.3. Market Capitalization

Firm	Market Cap. (billion dollars) As of December 2006	Year Incorporated	Average (since established) market valuation
Gen Electric	363,57	1879	2,86
Microsoft	286,36	1975	9,24
Procter Gamble	201,25	1837	1,19
Google	149,10	1998	18,64
IBM	142,32	1888	1,21
Walt Disney	70,74	1923	0,85
Gen Motors	17,05	1908	0,17
Ford	14,51	1903	0,14

The table above gives the market capitalization for a sample of large firms and the number of years since incorporation. The last column is a measure of the average market valuation since the incorporation of each firm (market capitalization/number of years since incorporation). As the results from the table clearly demonstrate Google is by far the firm which has added the most market value since establishment.

10 Mapping the Integrated Innovation Space: A Look at the Mirror

> Mirror, mirror, on the wall,
> Who in this land is fairest of all?
> The mirror answered:
> You, my queen, are fair; it is true.
> But the young queen
> Is a thousand times fairer than you.

Snow White and the Seven Dwarfs, *Jacob and William Carl Grimm*

10.1 Innovation Diagnostics

There exist a significant number of diagnostics tools that could be employed to evaluate and understand an organization's strengths and weaknesses in the field of innovation management. One basic motivation of the use of these tools is that such diagnostics permit the manager to assess the *gap* that exists, whether it be with respect to its competitors or an internal gap - that between its innovation capacity and desired innovation goals (including the organizational preparedness).

In this chapter we discuss some of innovation mapping methods that exist as well as introduce some diagnostics tools that are used with the Integrated Model. The mapping (innovation diagnostics) in the integrated space can be used for determining:

- Where is the product (single product firm) in the archetype space?
- Where are the competitors?
- Assesment *gaps*, using various intra firm metrics (for instance is the customer's perspective of the innovativeness of the product different from the firm's?)
- How do the market outcome enjoyed by the firm different from its closest rivals?

- Whether the innovation strategy bearing fruit?
- How close is the organizational culture to culture demanded by the market archetype a firm is in[1]?

This chapter is organized as follows – in Sect. 10.2 we discuss some firm level diagnostics employed by consultants and also macro innovation meaures. Sect. 10.3 presents some general measurement issues in innovation diagnostics in the integrated space. The internal diagnostics used in mapping the integrated innovation space is presented in Sect. 10.4 followed in Sect. 10.5 where the three types of mapping in the integrated innovation space are presented.

10.2 How Management Consultants Do It

In their book, *Making Innovation Work*, authors Davila, Epstein and Shelton[2] defend an approach to metrics that they call *the balanced scorecard for innovation*. According to these authors:

> "A basic tenet of the balanced scorecard is that the measurement system is only as good as the underlying business model. The business model describes how the company will be innovative and how it will generate value from innovation [...] The richer our understanding of the innovation processes, the better our business model will be and the derived measurement system will provide a more informed management of innovation. By making the business case for innovation investments, managers can integrate innovation impacts into their business strategies."

The innovation balanced scorecard employs a business model that focuses on four key areas – *inputs, processes, outputs* and *outcome*:

Inputs are resources devoted to the innovation effort. The resources include personnel, money, infrastructure and time. Besides explicit measures, the scorecard attempts to include intangibles like motivation and corporate culture.

---

[1] The last issue regarding measurement of organizational capacity for innovation management and the organizational culture in general is not addressed in this chapter and is beyond the scope of this book. Some organizational aspects are addressed in chapter 11.
[2] See Davila et al. (2005).

Processes involve the use and transformation of inputs into outputs. Thus the organization's creative processes, project execution as well as integrated execution (the latter tracks aggregate performance of all projects).

Outputs measures are the result of innovation efforts are focused on key characteristics such as whether the company has superior R&D performance, more effective customer acquisition or better customer loyalty. The indicators used by the authors in the innovation balanced score card (area of outputs) include:

> "...technology leadership (number of patents, seminars, technology licenses and percentage of technology adoption in the business model), project completion (measured against expectations or competitors), new product introduction (number of successful products, their acceptance versus competitors, market share and sales), business process improvement (improvement in processed metrics) and market leadership (customer acquisition, customer share and customer loyalty)."

Outcome measures employed in the innovation balanced score card differ from outputs in that they describe value creation. The outcome measures attempt to capture how innovation effort is translated from outputs into value for the company as well as the net amount of the value contribution.

The innovation metrics designed by the Davila et. al. emphasize that the business model cannot be rigid and needs to vary based on different types of innovation and business processes.

Muller, Välikangas, and Merlyn (2005) take a somewhat different approach to innovation metrics, using capability, resource and resource views to come up with a metrics that can *assess and develop a company's capacity for innovation*. The authors explain each view as follows:

> "*Resource view.* Companies must balance optimization (tactical investment in the existing business) and innovation (strategic investment in new businesses). The resource view addresses the allocation of resources to effect this balance. The resource inputs are capital, labour, and time. Output is the return on investment in strategic innovation.
> *Capability view.* The capability view assesses the extent to which the company's competencies, culture, and conditions support the conversion of innovation resources (see resource view) into opportunities for business renewal. The inputs of this capability view are the preconditions

for innovation, i.e. the extent to which a company's skills, tools, culture, and values are adapted to innovation. For example, does the company consider past demonstrations of innovativeness when selecting new recruits? Outputs include the development of new skills and knowledge domains that spawn innovation as well as the number of strategic options (i.e. opportunities to significantly advance an existing business or invest in a new business).

Leadership view. The leadership view assesses the degree to which a company's leadership supports innovation. As such, it evaluates leaders' involvement in innovation activities, the establishment of formal processes to promote innovation, and dissemination of innovation goals."

Innovation processes (such as incubators, innovation markets, venture funds, and innovation incentives) interlink with the resource view and the capability view, as suggested in the Fig. 10.1 below.

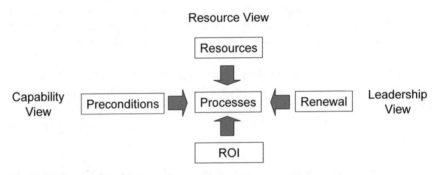

Fig. 10.1. Innovation framework

Other authors and consultants have devised different sets of diagnostics, depending upon measurement objectives and the conceptual model on which the metrics are based. For instance the consulting firm *Innosight*[3] has devised a set of diagnostics based upon Clayton Christensen's concept of disruptive innovation.

Their diagnostics are based on four basic principles – focusing on what firm wants to do, be attentive to consumer needs, how to be attractive for the worst clients and understanding where consumption is constrained. Thus they come up with three different diagnostics[4].

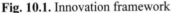

[3] http://www.innosight.com/
[4] http://hbswk.hbs.edu/item/4300.html

Customer diagnostic, tries to identify possible *disruptable* markets. This is done using the following indicators: "people complaining about overly complex, expensive products and services", "features that are not valued and therefore are not used" and "decreasing price premiums for innovations that historically created value". Attentions should be paid to non-consumers in each market.

The second diagnostic is the *portfolio diagnostic*. This assesses whether potential innovations could have success in a market, "looking at the technological characteristics of the innovation and at the potential business model by which the innovation might be brought to market."

The third and final diagnostic is the *competitor diagnostic*. This assesses competitors to "ensure that the selected opportunity takes unique advantage of their weaknesses and blind spots". This diagnostic analyzes whether competitors respond to a new innovation.

For purposes of international comparisons, there exist **macro measures of innovation** using firm level surveys. These measure innovation capacities, efforts as well as outcomes for different economies. One innovation index is applied to the OECD countries (see also Box 1.3 in Chap. 1). The **Oslo Manual** provides definitions and methodologies used in collecting data on *corporate strategies*, the *role of diffusion, sources of innovative ideas and obstacles to innovation, inputs to innovation, the role of public policy in industrial innovation, the outputs of innovation, and the impacts of innovation* (Archibugi and Sirilli, 2001). The categories of information collected are:

- prevalence of the innovation (number of firms, industries);
- types of innovation (products, processes);
- goals of innovation (improved or radically new product, new market, higher quality, better performance);
- internal sources of innovation (in-house R&D, sales and marketing, management);
- external sources of innovation (suppliers, clients, university or government laboratories, technical literature);
- practices for protecting innovations (patents, trademarks, trade secrets, complexity of industrial design);
- intensity of innovation (ongoing, occasional);
- obstacles to innovation (lack of skilled personnel, high risk, lack of information, regulatory barriers);

- impact on workers (number of employees, productivity, skills); and impact on economic performance (percentage of sales attributable to new or improved products or processes) (see Hansen, 2001).

Most measures of innovation use outcome data, focusing mostly on product innovation, where outcome is measured by the number of *patents*. Indeed in one reader survey by the R&D Magazine, the single largest measure chosen by the readers to measure an organization's success in innovation was the "ability of a new product to solve a customer's problem." The number of patents obtained by the organization as a historical measure of an organization's success in innovation was listed in the survey after other product-based measures of innovation as shown in Fig. 10.2.

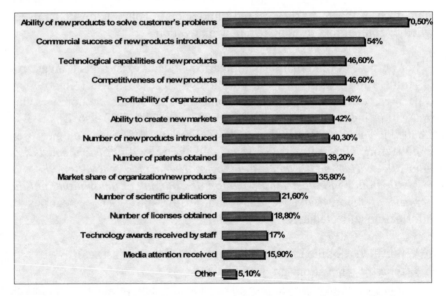

Fig. 10.2. How do you measure your organization's success in innovation?

The obsession with product based innovation measures (owing largely to a Schumpeterian view of innovation), is confirmed by a report by the National Academy of Sciences[5] (NAS). According to this report, "innovation measures must cover five activities:

- the introduction to the market of new products;

---

[5] Brown et al. (2004).

- the development of new processes to produce or deliver products to the market;
- the funding of new sources of supply of raw materials;
- the development of new markets; and
- changes in the organization of firms."

The report by the NAS includes other measures besides R&D for measuring innovation, as following:

> "The main activities involved in innovation are, in addition to R&D, other acquisition of knowledge (patents, licenses, and technical services); acquisition of machinery and equipment (both incorporating new technology and for standard use when producing a new product); various other preparations for production and delivery, including tooling up and staff training; and internal and external marketing aimed at the introduction of the innovation."

10.3 *Who's Who* – Diagnostics in the Integrated Model

The Integrated Model and the associated dynamic analyses can be a powerful tool for both management consultants as well as managers, permitting not just a look at the mirror, but also as a first step to designing effective strategy. Using a set of mapping tools one can locate a product (or single product firm) in one of the four market archetypes – the *wolf*, the *bear*, the *fox* and *sheep*. The mapping is executed for the entire integrated innovation space and not just the archetype space. A mapping of organizational mismatch is also permitted by the Integrated Model diagnostics, which estimates the *gap* between organizational capabilities and product organizational demands as well as the organizational needs that need to be aligned to innovation ambitions. The organizational challenges are discussed in Chap. 11.

Some caveats are in order with regards to mapping of a product in the integrated innovation space. Some of these caveats hold not just for the integrated innovation diagnostics, but for all mapping of this nature. It should be noted that exercises of innovation metrics are as good as the underlying model (when it exists) and the choice of the variables that describe the model.

First, one should take into account the temporal dimension of any characterization exercise due to changing internal dynamics as well as external business environment. A product identified today as a fox for instance can very quickly morph into sheep. Thus a **continuous mapping exercise** gives a truer picture of archetypical characterization.

Second, for purposes of measurement, one should exercise extreme **care in the choice of variables** used to measure each dimension (competitive pressure, degree of innovation/product differentiation and market outcomes). Although the literature in industrial organization, strategy, or innovation can serve as a guide, the literature far from arriving at any consensus on the best measurement tools for either competitive pressure or the degree of innovation[6].

Most innovation diagnostics generally suffer from an **absence of any theoretical framework** on which to base the survey questions. Diagnostics tend to be based on what the consultant believes as important for organizations to possess in order to produce innovative products, which is often a wish list of an organization's must haves. This leaves the door open to interpretation by the consultant, where his or her experience plays an important role. When any explicit underlying model does exist, they tend to be largely conceptual in nature.

Even when there is a guiding framework in the form of a model, the choice of the variables to represent a particular dimension is not without its critics. Measurement issues can prove to be a big stumbling block, in any mapping exercise. Competitive pressure can be measured for instance, using the number of firms in the industry or the degree of concentration of similar product firms. But neither measure may capture the true *competitive heat* felt by firms. A measure of concentration for instance may indicate that there is little industry concentration, yet the true competition a firm feels may come from global competitors. This is especially true in the manufacturing sector in today's globalized economies. Another measure of competitive pressure might be to use the price elasticity of demand, with products lying to the right of the archetype space having more elastic demand curves.

A further problem with mapping lies in the **credibility of responses** received if the mapping tool is based on survey questions. Our approach has been to use a diagnostic tool, albeit subjective (depends on who is

---

[6] In the previous section we presented three examples of innovation metrics. A search on the web reveals many other metrics used by consultants often without any theoretical or model underpinnings.

responding!) uses what we believe to be a judicious mix of variables to locate a product along each dimension. We try *to **minimize the margin of error*** arising from interpretation and at the same time ***maximize the information content*** of the responses.

With the integrated innovation framework in place, the mapping challenge is to position a single product firm (or a product or service) in each one of the four spaces- the archetype space, the strategy space, the outcome space and the market space. Complete diagnostics consist of ***three different and complementary sources of information***. The most important is a set of internal diagnostics in the form of a survey questionnaire. A second set is an external survey, principally for clients of the same and similar products as well as suppliers. The third set consists of using external (mostly macro) indicators which include sectorial studies (Fig. 10.3).

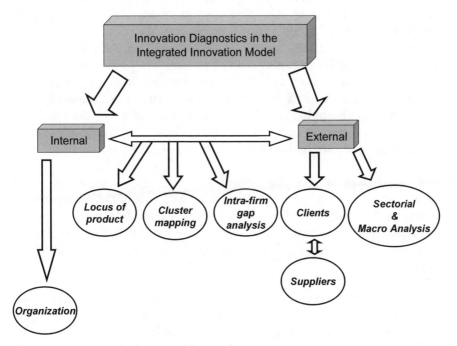

Fig. 10.3. Mapping the integrated innovation space

In the following section we provide an overview of the first set of diagnostics, the **internal diagnostics** using survey questions to map values in each of the three dimensions – degree of market pressure, degree of innovation-product differentiation and market outcomes. There are three types of mapping made possible by the internal diagnostics, which we also explain in the next section.

10.4 Mapping the Integrated Innovation Space – A Look at the Mirror

The internal diagnostics we have designed consists of a set of thirty questions that maps the position of a firm in the integrated innovation space. The basic thrust of this diagnostic is not so much as a metrics for innovation[7], but to serve as a measurement tool to capture which of the four market archetypes a product is in and what are the outcomes of the innovation-differentiation strategy pursued.

The internal diagnostics, in conjunction with the external data, permits **three types of mapping**. The first consists of mapping the **locus of a product** (or single product firm) in the integrated innovation space (archetype space, strategy space, outcome space and the market space). The second is **cluster mapping**, whereby, comparisons and benchmarking can be performed between a product (single product firm) with regards to a group of competing products (firms). The third set of mapping is an **intrafirm-gap mapping**, which permits the firm to analyze and understand divergences between variables within a particular dimension. All the three types are enabled by the same set of survey questions.

A fourth type of mapping relates to organizational capabilities and needs, and is enabled by the internal diagnostics, that of the organizational mismatch. This estimates the 'gap' between organizational capabilities and the organisation's demands for innovation. Note that for mapping of organizational alignment (Chap. 11, Sect. 11.3), only an internal survey is used.

The following sub sections present the mapping tools (internal diagnostics) for each of the three dimensions (or four if two outcome dimensions are considered, which we eschew here).

---

[7] A thorough innovation metrics should address first what sort of innovation is being measured (architectural, modular etc. if product innovation). In our case, the metrics is not of innovation per se, but of product positioning in the integrated innovation space.

10.4.1 Degree of Market Pressure

As had been mentioned in the previous section, the degree of market pressure is a dimension that is often difficult to measure (as is indeed innovation or the degree of product differentiation). An objective way to measure market pressure could be to use the number of firms in the industry or concentration measures. However that is fraught with some danger as we had mentioned in the previous section. To accurately measure the competitive pressure, simply taking into account the number of local (or national) suppliers is not enough. A true measure would have to include global suppliers as well, especially for manufactured goods (and now increasingly IT related services). Another objective measure could also include some concentration measures[8]. Given that the diagnostic map we have devised requires responses from the firms (internal survey) and hence subjective in nature, an ideal diagnostic could include both objective (sectorial) analyses as well as responses from the internal survey.

For the internal survey, (the auto diagnostic performed by managers in the firm), to capture the degree of competition we use a mix of four variables-*competitive pressure* (as felt by the manager), *entry barriers, degree of product choice available to consumers, and the price pressure* (degree of freedom in setting product price).

Table 10.1 summarizes the measurement objective of each of the four variables intended to measure competitive market pressure.

Table 10.1. Measurement objectives in diagnostics of competitive pressure dimension.

Variable measured	Measurement objective
Competitive pressure	How much is the market pressure felt by the firm?
Entry barriers	How easy is it for firms to enter the industry?
Consumer options	Do consumers have many competitive options for the product?
Price pressure	How much control does the firm have in setting product price?

---

[8] For instance using either the Herfindahl index or the Gini coefficient. The Herfindahl index uses the square of market share as an indicator of the degree of concentration in a market, scaled between 0 (high degree of competition) and 1 (no competition). The Gini coefficient is a measure of inequality of a distribution, with a score of 0 corresponding to perfect equality and 1 corresponding to perfect inequality.

Some sample questions included in the diagnostic to measure the degree of competitive pressure include the following:

- Our market is characterized by: few competitors (0); many competitors (10).

- In terms of the functionalities of our product, there is: no substitute in the market: (0); many substitutes (10).

- Our market is characterized by: low turbulence in terms of entry or exit of firms (0); new firms are constantly entering the market and in general there is high market turbulence (10).

- In terms of our pricing strategy: We are price followers and the market dictates the price we can set (0); we have freedom in setting the price for our product (10).

- Our price: is not under pressure, indeed price is not the buyer's principal decision variable(0); is constantly under great pressure (10).

- The price we set is: slightly above production costs(0); there is a comfortable margin over production costs (10).

Fig. 10.4 below presents the format in which the sample questions appear in the survey.

Note that the scaling (from 0 to 10) is designed to elicit *intuitive responses*. Note too that the value of a response need not necessarily correspond to a *low-high* scale but may be the exact inverse. Case in point is the last question above. This is also true for some questions in other dimensions as well.

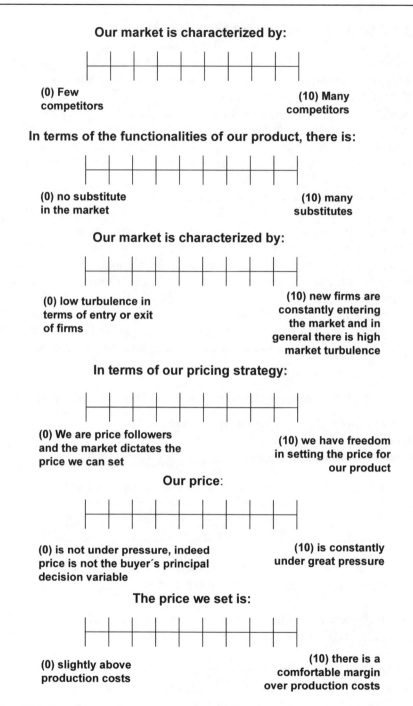

Fig. 10.4. Sample questions to gauge competitive pressure

10.4.2 Innovation-Product Differentiation

Similar to the diagnostic of the degree of market pressure, we use a mix of measures (variables) to capture the degree of innovation/product differentiation. As discussed earlier in Sect. 10.3, there are some macro measures of innovation, which attempt to compare the 'innovativeness' or innovative capacities of different countries. Most of these studies are based on firm level surveys and as we had noted, patents and intellectual properties of an organization find prominence is innovation measures.

As in the other dimensions, we again use a combination of variables that attempt to capture the extent to which a *product is innovative and different from competitors* and to some extent *the innovation capacity of the firm.* The variables chosen are the following - degree of innovation as viewed by the firm, consumer perception of product differentiation, the degree to which the product is protected from 'me too' products, consumer's perception of the degree of differentiation, and finally innovation investments made. Again as with the other two dimensions, the questions may vary if applied to a service sector or not, as well as the weights assigned to each question to measure the value along any dimension.

Table 10.2. Measurement objectives in diagnostics of the innovation dimension

Variable measured	Measurement objective
Differentiation	How differentiated is the product?
Product protection	To what extent is there protection from the product being copied?
Costumer's perception	How differentiated does the client feel of the product being offered?
Investments	How much investment input has been made towards innovation?

Below are some questions that we include in the diagnostic to measure the degree of innovation-product differentiation:

- Our product is defined as having: standard, modular attributes (0); specialized features that are often proprietary (10).

- We believe that: there are many firms who are providing something very similar to ours (0); our offer is really new representing a radical departure from any other firms'(10).

- We believe that we offer to clients products that are: inferior to the competitors' products (0); much better than our competitors' products (10).

- Our products are: not dependent on any protection (0); protected by patent/copyrights/any special knowledge (10).

- Our products: are not difficult to be copied (0); are not easily duplicated by other firms (10).

- Our brand: plays a very small role in the customers mind when making product purchase (0); strongly influences and is decisive for the client (10).

- The type of persons we need in our enterprises are: easy of recruit and doesn't demand much qualification (0); is difficult to recruit and demand additional training (10).

- To maintain our market position: we don't need great investments in technology or personnel (0); we have to invest constantly in new ideas and technology to maintain our market position (10).

Fig. 10.5 illustrates the presentation to the respondent of these questions, intended to measure the degree of innovation-product differentiation.

Porter's contribution in this regard was important in framing some of the questions to measure the innovation dimension[9].

---

[9] See Porter (1998). For instance Porter takes into account factors such as the creative skills of employees, the different product characteristics, and the investments made towards continuous improvement and innovation of products. Certain ideas expressed by Kaplan and Norton (2004) have also been helpful in designing the survey.

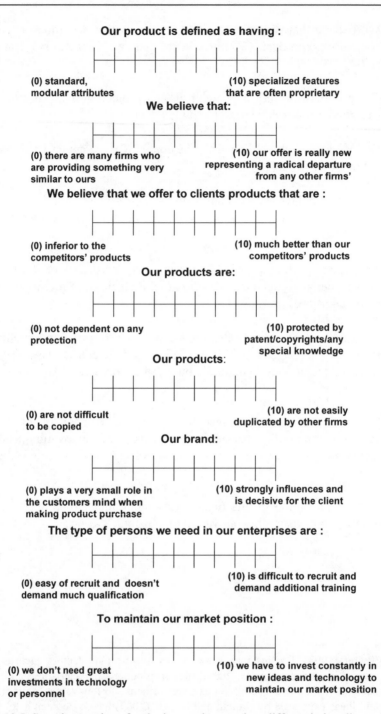

Our product is defined as having :

(0) standard,
modular attributes

(10) specialized features
that are often proprietary

We believe that:

(0) there are many firms who
are providing something very
similar to ours

(10) our offer is really new
representing a radical departure
from any other firms'

We believe that we offer to clients products that are :

(0) inferior to the
competitors' products

(10) much better than our
competitors' products

Our products are:

(0) not dependent on any
protection

(10) protected by
patent/copyrights/any
special knowledge

Our products:

(0) are not difficult
to be copied

(10) are not easily
duplicated by other firms

Our brand:

(0) plays a very small role in
the customers mind when
making product purchase

(10) strongly influences and
is decisive for the client

The type of persons we need in our enterprises are :

(0) easy of recruit and doesn't
demand much qualification

(10) is difficult to recruit and
demand additional training

To maintain our market position :

(0) we don't need great
investments in technology
or personnel

(10) we have to invest constantly in
new ideas and technology to
maintain our market position

Fig. 10.5. Sample questions for the innovation-product differentiation dimension

10.4.3 Market Outcome(s)

As we had seen earlier in Chap. 3, the market outcome of a firm in its competitive environment can be variously represented by its sales, market share, margins or profits. We can use either **one market outcome dimension** in the integrated innovation space **or two**, with the latter implying that the outcome space (third quadrant of the model) is characterized by the two outcome dimensions with a behavioural relationship between them determined by concave curves in this third quadrant (if the variables were market share and profits).

If only one dimension, that of simply *market outcome* is used, then we suggest the use of three variables. Table 10.3 summarizes the measurement objective of each of these three variables.

Table 10.3. Measurement objectives din the diagnostics of the market outcome dimension

Variable measured	Measurement objective
Market return	How is the market return?
Financial performance	In terms of financial performance of your product, are you satisfied?
Consumer perception	Are the clients satisfied with your product?

Some sample questions included in the diagnostic to measure the unique dimension of market outcome, include the following:

- Our market share is: low and under constant pressure (0); high and stable (10).

- With regards to new markets: at the moment our objective is simply to survive (0); we are always trying to expand and explore new opportunities in markets (10).

- Our clients pay for our products: less than for our competitors' products (0); more than for our competitors' products (10).

- Our margins before taxes are: small and under constant pressure (0); are comfortable and above industry average (10).

- With respects to our investments: we make few investments and even if we did, it wouldn't pay off (0); we make large investments and are satisfied with the returns from those investments (10).

- We are: concerned with our low sales (0); satisfied with the regular increments of sales (10).

- Our products: have less prestige than our competitors (0); enjoy much more prestige than our competitors (10).

- Our clients' are: disappointed and may easily switch to our rivals products if we are not careful (0); very satisfied with what we have to offer (10).

Some additional caveats are in order here with regards to market outcome. **First** note that market outcome so measured, includes customer satisfaction. However if we wish to measure only financial returns and market returns such as market share, profit margins, sales or profits, then questions intended to measure customer satisfaction can either be dropped or assigned a negligible weight in the final mapping. **Second**, if two market return dimensions are being measured, then the first set would include questions related to market share and the second to profits (or margins). **Third**, in measuring market outcome, in general new products or new processes are excluded in the subjective analyses given that our experience has led us to conclude that in a survey setting, the *newness* was subject to multiple interpretations, especially in the service sector. However in the objective diagnostics as well as more on site consultations would include this variable (new products, processes, markets, raw materials, marketing etc).

Fig. 10.6 illustrates the presentation to the respondent of these questions, to measure market outcome (generic).

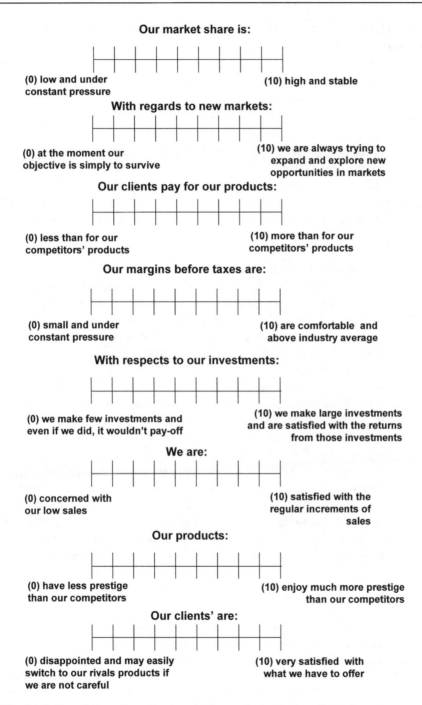

Fig. 10.6. Sample questions to measure the market outcome dimension

10.5 Three Types of Mapping in the Integrated Innovation Space

The set of thirty survey[10] questions included in our internal diagnostics permits three types of mapping, besides mapping of the organization alignment. The first enables the mapping the locus of a product (or single product firm) in the integrated innovation space. The second is cluster mapping, which permits comparisons and benchmarking to be performed between a product (single product firm) and a group of competing products (firms). The third set of mapping is intrafirm-gap analyses, which permit the firm to analyze and understand divergences between variables within a particular dimension. All the three types are enabled by the same set of survey questions.

1. **Locus of a product in the integrated innovation space:** The set of questions contained in the survey enable us to find the location of a product or a firm (if single product) in the integrated innovation space comprising of the archetype space, the strategy space, the outcome space and the market space. Fig. 10.7 illustrates an example of the mapping in the integrated innovation space, of a fox whose product enjoys a market niche.

2. **Cluster Mapping** uses cumulative information previously retrieved from products in the same sector and activity which permits comparisons and benchmarking to be performed between the product and a group of competing products. The information presented with regards to other firms can either be the averages of the information relating to the firms in the same sector or simply of one best performing firm in that sector, or both. Fig. 10.8 presents the graphical representation of such cluster mapping. The cluster mapping enables the firm to know its relationship with respect other firms in the industry thereby enabling more detailed benchmarking analyses and autodiagnostics.

---

[10] The choice of thirty questions was based upon our quest for maximizing the information content but not be too lengthy that may trigger of non responses or incorrect responses. We believe our current choice of questions satisfy this criteria. However for a detailed analyses, the number of questions extended to the extent possible consistent with the variables and dimensions being measured.

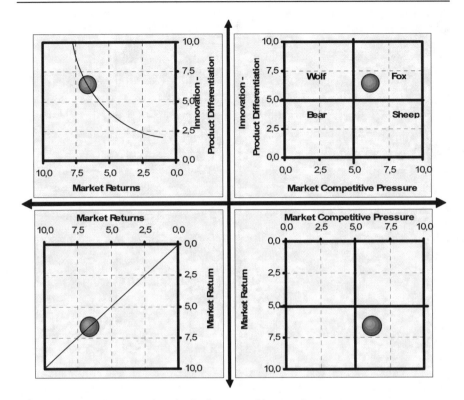

Fig. 10.7. Locating a product in the integrated innovation space

Fig. 10.8 illustrates an example of cluster mapping, with the firm (small ball), the cluster (medium ball) and the market leader (large ball). The market leader is the product which has the highest returns in the sector (and is most differentiated).

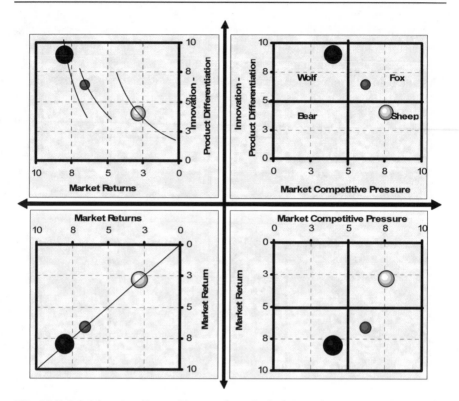

Fig. 10.8. Locating a product with regards to the industry cluster. Legend: grey small bubble – product (single product firm); white medium bubble – industry; large black bubble – leader

3. **Intrafirm-gap mapping** permit the manager to analyze and understand divergences between variables within a particular dimension. Comparison is performed 'internally' where for a given dimension; the averages of the variables are compared after taking into account the standard deviation of the values obtained of the different variables in the dimension.

Let us take the example of our product, a fox close to the wolf archetype (Fig. 10.9 below). The product is in an environment where there is competition without it being intense. On closer inspection however, one finds that although the manager believes that there are few competitors in the marketplace, the consumers perceive that there are other options available.

Significant discrepancies in the values of variables in the same dimension clearly call for the attention of the manager. Following the example above, the manager is alerted to the need to be both aware of the mismatch in the perception of competition as well as devise strategies to deal with such a situation.

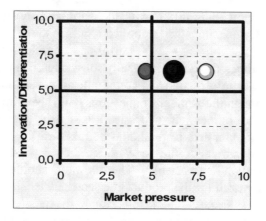

Fig. 10.9. Intra-firm gap mapping. Legend: black bubble – product (single product firm); white bubble – clients perception of competition; grey bubble – manager's belief of market competition

Fig. 10.10 presents all the three previous diagnostic in just one figure.

Some final considerations are in order here. With regards to the final mapping of a product or a single product firm, we suggest or highlight the following approaches, (which we have applied in our own diagnostics for over a thousand different firms).

- Some questions are repeated, either because the same question can be applicable to measure two different variables in the same dimension or two different dimensions (for instance a question on client perception used in estimating both market pressure as well as product differentiation). However the weights assigned to repeated questions need not be the same.
- In general, unless there are compulsive reasons to do so, weights have generally been uniform across all questions.
- The more responses obtained from within an organization, the more reliable is the diagnostic.
- Intra firm diagnostics is enabled by checking how the mean scores of different variables for the same dimension compare.

If values are significantly different, then that should act as a red flag to the firm, as an issue that the manager has to address.

- Statistical rules are applied to identify inconsistencies in responses (for instance if a score was more than two standard deviations away from the average value of a particular dimension.)

- Questions may differ, with inclusion and substitution by other survey questions when applied to a firm in the service sector.

- True mapping has to be performed continuously or at least a few times in a year, especially for products in the fast evolving areas of information and communications technology.

- Although the number of questions have been limited to thirty, if both resources and necessity arises then this number can be easily extended. Care should be taken in the choosing of new questions, and the questions should best represent the corresponding variables. The questions should (could) also be customized for the product and sector under study.

- Whenever possible, for thorough diagnostic field visits and interviews by the consultant are strongly encouraged.

- The best diagnostic tools work in tandem - the internal diagnostics, feedback from the external surveys and field visits and interviews.

Thus while diagnostics exist at the firm level, both those which use an explicit conceptual framework and others without, the diagnostics permitted in the integrated innovation space can be a source of valuable empirical information for the manager. In this chapter we discussed internal diagnostics enabled by applying a brief survey to employees in a firm. The three types of diagnostics explained in this section - locus of a product, cluster mapping and intrafirm – gap mapping (besides organizational diagnostics), can provide the firm with a complete set of tools for strategy analysis. In combination with external data for more objective input, as well as field visits and interviews, the manager can have not just a very good diagnostics of the organization's position in the innovation space, but also opens the door to the understanding of many *why's*. The diagnostics also prepare the manager to understand future dynamics given the benefits of using the integrated framework.

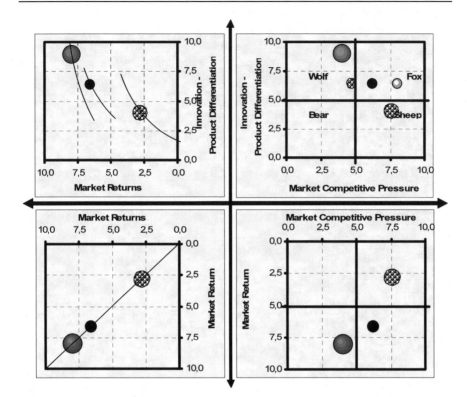

Fig. 10.10. Complete diagnostic. Legend: black bubble – product (single product firm); white bubble – clients perception of competition; black and white small bubble – manager's belief of market competition; grey bubble – market leader; black and white big bubble – industry

11 An Integrated Innovation Landscape

Over the next two years, two-thirds of
corporate CEOs say they're going to need to
make fundamental changes to their business.

The reasons, they say, are many: intensified
competition, escalating customer expectations,
and unexpected market shifts. For many, you
can add to that list workforce issues,
technological advances, regulatory concerns,
and globalization.

Yet fewer than half of CEOs think their
organizations have handled such changes with
much success in the past.

Expanding the Innovation Horizon, Global CEO Study 2006

11.1 Innovation Management

Writing about innovation strategy or management innovation is beyond the scope of this book. Nor is it the goal. We have presented a new framework for analyses that permits the academic, the management consultant and the manager alike to understand *where* a product (or a single product firm) is located in the integrated innovation space, *why* it is so located and which then provides valuable clues as to *what* to do while designing strategy. The integration of the important determinant variables in one visual framework with a robust and an internally consistent theoretical basis also permits a rich analysis of many market dynamics. The Integrated Model is an important step towards devising comprehensive firm strategy.

While innovation diagnostics permitted by the model can serve as an important tool for the manager, we have so far eschewed from dwelling on management and innovation strategy. In this chapter however, we discuss some issues relating to innovation strategy. This chapter starts with a broad sweep of the innovation landscape from the strategy perspective. Sect. 11.2 presents some important survey results on how a CEO view the innovation horizon. We then discuss what we believe to be two fundamental strategy related issues with regards to innovation and market outcome – innovation payoff and having an innovation ready organization.

11.2 The Innovation Horizon

In a recent survey conducted by IBM′s Global Business Service, 765 CEOs, business executives and public sector leaders from around the world were asked on their plans and perspectives on innovation. The 64 page report entitled *Expanding the Innovation Horizon*, Global CEO Study 2006, makes clear that, business model innovation mattered more than ever and that external collaboration was considered indispensable. Moreover, the survey participants felt that for an organization to be innovative, *orchestration* was required from the top. Among the report's findings were the following[1]:

- **Business model innovation was becoming the new strategic differentiator.** The report noted that companies that had grown their operating margins faster than their competitors, were putting twice as much emphasis on business model innovation as underperformers.
- **Business model innovation can pay off**. Firms that were putting twice as much emphasis on business model innovation as underperformers had grown their operating margins faster than their competitors.
- **Sources of innovation**. The surveyed CEOs reported that their company's employees were the most significant source for innovative ideas. But ranking close behind employees were business partners and customers. Thus indicating that two out of the three top sources for the best ideas now lie outside the enterprise. Indeed top performers used external sources 30% more than underperformers.
- **Collaboration pays off.** Companies with higher revenue growth reported using external sources significantly more than the slower growers. Around 76% of the CEOs surveyed ranked business partnerships and collaboration as top sources of new ideas.
- **It pays to pay the innovators**. Firms that reward their employees who contribute towards the organization's innovation, get rewarded from

---

[1] For a summary of the report, go to IBM's web site: www.ibm.com

such incentives. The report found that companies who rewarded individual innovation contributions saw:

There was an increase in revenues by 2.5% more than companies who did not.

Increased operating margin by 2% more than companies who did not reward individual innovation contributions.

Fig. 11.1 summarizes the innovation areas considered most important by the respondents, including those from the public sector.

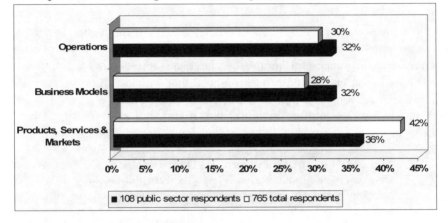

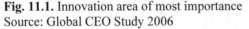

Fig. 11.1. Innovation area of most importance
Source: Global CEO Study 2006

As noted earlier, business model innovation is finding a new and important place as a differentiator. According to the report:

"CEOs were candid about the need to search out new competitive differentiators – even if that meant confronting a sacrosanct business model. "In the operations area, much of the innovation and cost savings that could be achieved has already been achieved. Our greatest focus is on business model innovation, which is where the greatest benefits lie." "It's not enough to make a difference on product quality or delivery readiness or production scale. We must innovate in areas where our competition does not act – by developing new competencies and alliances." Global connectivity (created through telecommunications, IT infrastructure and open standards) makes new skills and partners accessible and practical to employ and enables entirely new forms of collaboration, and, thus, new business models. Of course, the same global connectivity also exposes firms to new competitors with very different business models and cost bases, which, in turn, can force business model innovation."

The Global CEO Study 2006 report suggests five steps that the CEO can take to expand the innovation horizon:

- Think broadly, act personally and manage the innovation mix;
- Make the business model substantially different;
- Ignite innovation through business and technology integration;
- Defy collaboration limits;
- Always force a look outside the organization.

What is perhaps one of the most crucial aspects of innovation is not just how to innovate or where to innovate, but **who is inspiring the innovation drive**. Highly successful innovators have an active CEO guiding and involved in the innovation process, a need that was identified by the IBM innovation report. As noted in a Business Week article, only a CEO can change a business culture at top speed, giving the example of Alan G. Lafley, Procter & Gamble CEO as well as innovator-in-chief[2].

> "Lafley sits in on all 'upstream' R&D review meetings, 15 a year, that showcase new products. He also spends three full days a year with the company's Design Board, a group of outside designers who offer their perspective on upcoming P&G products. "He's sort of the chief innovation officer", says P&G's Huston. "He's very, very involved." […] The CEO determines the culture. […] If the CEO is determined to [improve] the surfacing of ideas and determined to make critical choices, then the chances of an [organization's] figuring that out are much, much greater."

Without the enthusiasm and participation of top management in the innovation process, there is a strong likelihood that the innovation drive will sputter.

---

[2] See the article "The World's Most Innovative Companies, Business Week, 24th April 2006.

Box 11.1: How management innovation happens

Management guru, Gary Hamel says of management innovation as:

"…innovation in management principles and processes that ultimately changes the practice of what managers do, and how they do it. It is different from operational innovation; which is about how the work of transforming inputs into outputs actually gets done."

To read more visit the site: http://www.management-issues.com/2006/5/24/mentors/gary-hamel-management-innovation.asp

Writing in the Sloan Management Review, Birkinshaw and Mol (2006) state that "nothing about our current ways of working is inviolable." They studied more than 100 management innovations that took place over 130 years, arguing that despite its importance, management innovation is poorly understood and usually not systematically fostered. Of 12,774 peer-reviewed articles discussing technological innovation only 114 focused on management innovation—and few of the latter help businesses to improve their capacity for management innovation. Their research led the authors to conclude that management innovation typically goes through four stages:

- *dissatisfaction with the status quo*, resulting from a crisis, strategic threat, or operational problem (such as Motorola's development of Six Sigma)

- *inspiration from other sources*

- *invention* of the management innovation itself.

- *validation*, both internally and through external sources (by academics, consultants, media organizations, or industry associations.)

An interesting article on management practises, heralds "The world's most modern management – in India!" (see Kirkpatrick, 2006). In a broader culture to promote innovation, HCL has implemented some of the most innovative management practices. The article gives the example of how every employee rates their boss, their boss' boss, and any three other company managers they choose, on 18 questions using a 1-5 scale. Results are posted online for every employee to see! Every HCL employee can at any time create an electronic "ticket" to flag anything they think requires action in the company, which is then swiftly addressed by the management. By putting employees first, an Indian software giant is creating a culture that promotes participation, motivation and innovation.

11.3 An Integrated Innovation Strategy?

Throughout the course of this book, we have used the Integrated Innovation Model as the framework to analyze innovation and market outcome. Product characteristics based on the degree of innovation and competitive pressure described a product along four archetypes – the wolf, the bear, the fox and the sheep. Of fundamental relevance to the CEO is that it is not just *important to be different, but it must be worthwhile to do so*! While the different chapters in the book used the integrated innovation space to describe production positioning to market dynamics from – product life cycle to sustainability to mergers and acquisitions, it is instructive to point out some issues with strategic implications. So far we have deliberately eschewed from discussing management innovation strategy, focusing instead in presenting the Integrated Model and its potential to describe positioning and dynamics of products and firms. Nonetheless the Integrated Model can be used explicitly to study innovation strategy issues.

While this is a topic for future research, two issues relating to innovation strategy are discussed here. First is the necessity for innovation to deliver (discussed in this section). The second is on having the organization aligned with the market archetype a product is in and consistent with innovation goals (Sect. 11.4). The integrated innovation space serves as the framework for discussion.

11.3.1 It Is Not Just About Being a Wolf

The chances that a wolf would enjoy high market returns are greater than a fox and far greater than a sheep. Fig. 11.2 illustrates a wolf product enjoying high market returns. However it is important to remember the following:

1. It costs to be a wolf (*costs of innovation*)
2. It costs to remain a wolf (*sustainability of innovation*)
3. It pays to be a wolf. (*returns from innovation*)
4. You have to act a wolf (*organizational alignment*)

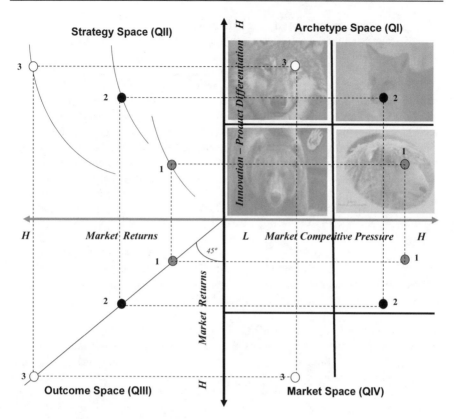

Fig. 11.2. Returns from innovation

While the returns from innovation are obvious with the wolf (3) enjoying high market returns, and treated to some extent in Chap. 1, we dwell briefly on the first two aspects of innovation and consequences for strategy. The organizational alignment issue is treated separately in the next section (Sect. 11.4).

Innovation is not easy – it costs to be a wolf and it costs to remain one. Innovation cannot be bought and spending on R&D is not enough. Writing in Strategy & Business, Kandybin and Kihn (2004) noted:

> "A decade ago, it would have been difficult to find a company less inventive than Levi Strauss. The storied jeans maker didn't need to be a pioneer: Its style was antistyle, and its durable denims all but sold themselves. Product development activities included basing a line of women's jeans on patterns designed for men. A price was paid, of course,

as competitors sensed and found ways to meet consumers' changing interests in denim. Between 1996 and 2001, Levi's sales fell from $7.1 to $4.3 billion.
When Philip A. Marineau was named CEO of the San Francisco–based company in late 1999, he offered up a one-word solution: *innovation*. Mr. Marineau was a vaunted "idea guy"; as head of PepsiCo Inc.'s North American business, he had championed the launch of Pepsi One cola, a product that revitalized Pepsi's lackluster diet segment. At Levi's, he wasted no time in dispatching designers to Europe and Asia to troll plazas and pachinko parlors for ideas. Spending on new product development increased, and a stream of new products began to roll off the apparel company's assembly line — Type 1 Jeans, Engineered Jeans, and the Dockers Mobile Pant, which sported pockets for cellular telephones, pagers, and PDAs.

A success story? Not quite: The new jeans, although popular overseas, never caught on in the U.S., and the Dockers Mobile Pant didn't mobilize consumers. Levi's announced a net loss of $40 million for the first half of 2003, and global sales fell to $1.8 billion.

Levi's is not alone. Academic and popular sources have been filling the business world with paeans to innovation. They have championed the search for the "new new thing," recommended the hiring of "cool hunters" who can uncover big profitable ideas, and suggested that companies can spend their way to novelty-premised growth. [...]

[...] Yet time and again, companies have found that spending more on innovation does not necessarily translate into accelerating sales, share, or profits. In 1995, Polaroid began pumping money into R&D in the core imaging business and significantly increased new product launches, but it was not enough to keep the company out of Chapter 11 in 2001. Maytag began making increases in R&D in 2001, yet through 2003 sales continued to slip."

The authors argue that incremental innovation investments are subject to diminishing returns and that there is an "innovation effectiveness curve." They suggest that this curve is concave, due to the diminishing marginal return on innovation investment (see Fig. 11.3).

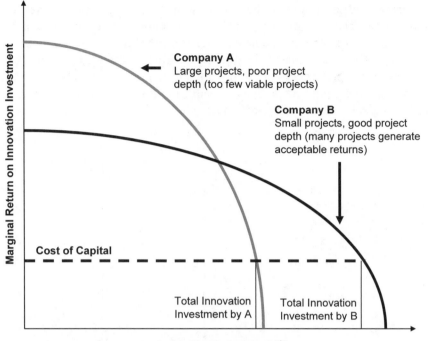

Fig. 11.3. The innovation effectiveness curve

Our concern regarding innovation strategy with an eye on results is obvious in the design of the Integrated Innovation Model, and indeed one of the motivations for our research which led to the framework. The introduction of markets and market outcome is made explicit in that they appear as two of the dimensions (or three of two market outcome dimensions are concerned) in the model.

The innovation payoff (IP) curves in the strategy space of the Integrated Model (see Chap. 3) demonstrate a slightly different trade-off. Recall that the IP curves represented *the return from activities associated with a given degree of market pressure, between the 'innovativeness' of a product and the market outcome.* Implicit in the construction of the curves is the diminishing returns from innovation effort. The concavity of the IP curves as we discussed in Chap. 3, reflected a similar diminishing return for incremental innovation. The elasticities of these curves determine the extent to which incremental innovation give results. The greater the elasticity the higher the market outcome of innovation.

Firms need to know that the elasticity of the payoff curves matter and innovation need not always payoff. Innovation-payoff curves which are inelastic (such as the one depicted as **II** in Fig. 11.4) would not yield the desired outcome and may indeed result in failure. Knowledge of markets and consumer preferences are important and failure of innovation to bring value to the consumers may result in disaster, no matter how technologically advanced your product is.

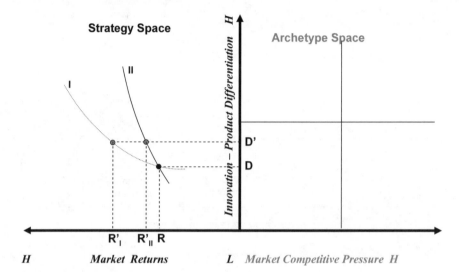

Fig. 11.4. Different innovation payoff curves

As we can se in Fig 11.4, the elasticity of the innovation payoff function plays an important role in the final outcome of an innovation. Both products depicted in the figure are at the same initial point (degree of differentiation **D** and result **R**). However, as the innovation payoff curve **I** is more elastic than **II**, an increase in the innovativeness of the product, fetches a much higher market return. As seen from the figure an equal increase of the degree of differentiation (**D'**), fetches different results.

While focused R&D is important, the sources for innovation today are much wider, reducing thus both innovation investment and effort as well as reducing risk. Tapping a much broader innovation base, "open innovation" (See Box 11.2) can be fundamental in this respect, increasing thereby the elasticity of the innovation payoff curve.

Although there is no single formula for innovation success, Jaruzelski et al. (2006) suggest that there are some common themes, and view the

innovation process to be a kind of value chain (Fig.11.5). The value chain suggested by the authors involves four interdependent elements:
- an ideation process (basic research and conception)
- project selection (the decision to invest)
- product development (in tune with the rest of the organization), and commercialization (bringing the product or service to market and a-dapting it to customer demands).

The authors hold that high-leverage companies (those that are able to successfully harness innovation investment) believe that besides being skilled in one particular stage they reinforce that skill with competence at all stages of the value chain. They also believe that some of the most successful innovators are more successful in the latter part of the innovation value chain, giving the example of Apple.

Organization and Culture

Processes and Tools

Fig. 11.5. Value chain of innovation process
Source: Jaruzelski et al. (2006)

Innovation has been so hyped up with management gurus exhorting "innovation as the only way out", it is difficult to not be caught up in the hype. But breaking out from the crowd, through the coming up with a new product or a novel process or a new business model, costs resources, from finance to intellectual. Sometimes the most desired outcomes need not come from radical innovations that mark clear departure from current processes or current product offerings, but may have more humble origins-that of redoing what exists, only better. Recall from our discussion on the Apple iPod (Chap. 6). iPod's wild success has its origins on existing technology. The iPod is an example of clever innovation standing on the shoulder giant of giants. Apple had made a previous attempt at radical innovation - the Apple Newton personal digital assistant. A radical innovation at that time with its raft of first time features failed dramatically in the eyes and hence the wallets of its customers. This radical innovation failed to provide value, neither to the consumer (and hence) nor to the producer. The case of the *Segway Human Transporter* that we had visited earlier in Chap. 5 (Box 5.2) is one of many products that have littered the innovation landscape, marked by disappointments.

The importance of sustaining your innovation has been mentioned variously and emphatically in this book, reflecting our research on how to protect innovation. Slowing the IP curves shift inwards and the braking the wolf or the fox slide into the commodity terrain of the sheep is every product manager and CEO's function.

Box 11.2: Open innovation

Time was that when you hit sixty five, or earlier, it was time to get the brochures out and head for Florida for retirement. Not any longer. While companies are starved for top quality people and given high costs of innovation effort with uncertain outcome, what better to tap these Florida seekers with years of experience? This is exactly the objective of YourEncore Inc., launched in late 2003, which aligns company's personnel needs with scientists and engineers with businesses, most of whom have retired from the research labs of large corporations, often with years of technical experience. Member companies, such as Procter & Gamble, Lilly or Boeing can hire these consultants to supplement their existing research personnel for particular projects.

Tapping outside for innovation, is fast gathering momentum among the most innovative companies. Smaller companies with little or no dedicated R&D centres have the potential to become leading innovators, tapping a worldwide source of innovation. The concept of open innovation was popularized by Chesbrough (2005) with the publication of an article on the open innovation concept in MIT's *Sloan Management Review*, along with a book titled *Open Innovation: The New Imperative for Creating and Profiting from Technology in 2003. Open innovation refers to* the broad concepts of leveraging external sources of ideas, technology and skilled power to drive innovation led growth. Some of the sources for open innovation can be "user led innovation" that we saw in Chap. 7 (Box 7.1).

Figs. 11.2a. and 11.2b, illustrate the closed and open innovation models (see www.pdma.org).

(continued)

Box 11.2: Open Innovation (cont.)

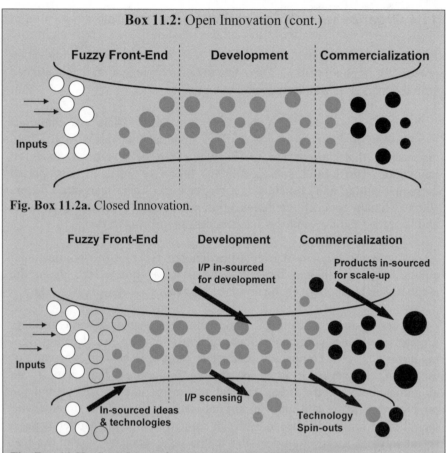

Fig. Box 11.2a. Closed Innovation.

Fig. Box 11.2b. Open Innovation

Companies such as Google are using the world as their R&D lab, constantly churning out "beta" products as users all over the world try them out on their keyboards, before deciding on which products to finally launch. Others such as IBM, the world's largest patent holder with more than 40000 patents are allowing free access to some of its patents and also funding the Open Initiative Project. IBM lets open source developers the royalty-free use of 500 of its 10,000 software related patents. This in the hope of creating a wider idea and product pool that it can tap in the future.

11.4 *Organovate* – Organization for Innovation

It is not enough to have an idea, a product, a market and an innovation process for implementation. There has to be an organization that is aligned with the market as well as the innovation goals.

"Innovation is easy", it is the doing that hurts! There are numerous impediments to innovation, and as IBM´s Global Innovation Study 2006 discovered, that current corporate culture can be a critical brake on innovation. The CEO's surveyed in the report felt that an unsupported corporate culture and climate was a bigger impediment than other factors (limited funding, workforce issues, process immaturity, inflexible physical and IT infrastructure and insufficient access to information).

Yet until recently, most executives ignored the role of organizational culture often considered the *soft* side of innovation effort, given the emphasis on technology as the driver of innovation.

Discussing an organizational culture and aspects such as team working, a creative climate, communications, responsibility etc., or defining right organizations for a company's product or market is beyond the scope of this book. However, it is of paramount importance that there is an alignment between the organizational culture on the one hand and the product positioning and innovation goals on the other. This alignment or lack thereof can be diagnosed in the Integrated Innovation Model, using a set of internal survey tools, similar to the three diagnostics that we had discussed in the previous chapter. We define here the right organization as one that demands two things:

- First, there has to be an alignment between the current design and orientation of the organization to the product in the market that it is in.
- Second there has to be an alignment with the innovation goals and the current corporate culture (of course there has also to be an alignment between innovation goals and the firm's resources). Below we briefly discuss each in turn.

11.4.1 Alignment: Archetype and Organization

Imagine a product that is a sheep, a *me too* commodity, with little to separate between itself and her many other competitors. What about the organization? What if the organization was geared towards production of fox products (Fig 11.6). Suppose that the organization is built around a culture which is not hierarchical, listening to clients, a directive management focused on innovation. While none of these organizational attributes are necessarily bad, are they necessarily right for a sheep archetype? Shouldn't the organizational focus for a product in this archetype be function driven, structured, concern for costs and productivity? A mismatch between the product's organization needs and the current organizational design and functioning means that resources are being wasted, and instead of the firm growing (as in the example above), the management practices currently followed could imply that the product could very soon be out of the market given the failure to ride the economies of scale and efficiency.

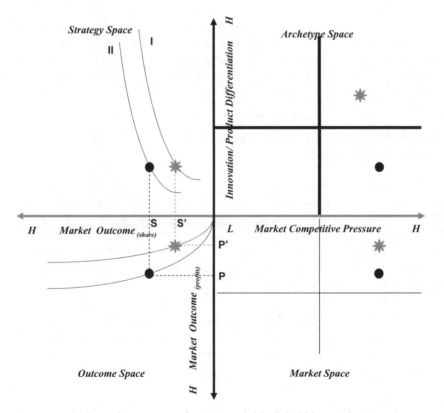

Fig. 11.6. A sheep that acts as a fox! Legend: black bubble: product; grey star: organization

As Fig. 11.6 illustrates, the mismatch between the current organization and product organizational needs resulting in the firm having a lower market share and profits (firm results **S'** and **P'** instead of **S** and **P** if there was no mismatch between the organization and product). This underperformance is a result of a mismatch- that of a sheep that acts like a fox.

Innovation payoff curve **I** reflects the reduced payoffs from misalignment due to the sheep product having a fox organization, leading to loss of focus and consequent inefficiencies as had been explained earlier. If there had been complete alignment, market share and profits would have been higher at **S** and **P** respectively, (corresponding to the **II** IP curve).

What is true in the example above is true for all market archetypes. There has to be an alignment between the current design and current functioning of the organization to the product in the market that it is in. Otherwise the organization is either stretched in the wrong direction or is lagging behind the organizational needs.

11.4.2 Alignment: Innovation Goals and Current Corporate Culture

So you want to break out from the pack and be a wolf? So what does it take to be a wolf? What are the demands of an organizational culture that is focused on innovation? Is your current organization capable of adapting to the organizational demands that requires a constant *supply* of fresh ideas for new products, personnel that is high motivated in a business environment that is very dynamic (sometimes even turbulent)? Is it a *listening organization*?

It is not enough to have the right idea, the right process, a new product for a new or emerging market. There has to be an organization that is capable of not just supporting such a product, but sustaining the churn of new product development.

A gap assessment of organizational needs for innovation and current organizational design for a company's that wants to be a wolf product, is essential. As essential as all the other elements that go into creating innovation - ideas, human resources, technology, innovative processes, design etc. While many authors have dealt with the question of what is the right organization for innovation[3], the positioning of the organizational requirements for innovation and current organizational design can be mapped via an assessment test in the integrated innovation space (Fig. 11.7)

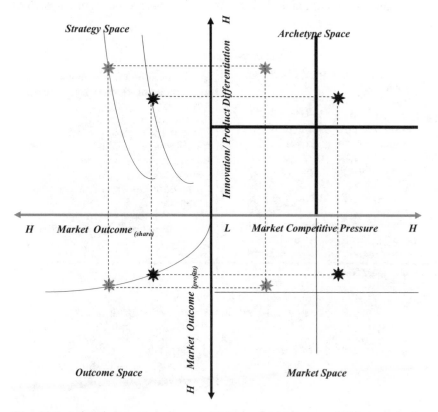

Fig. 11.7. A fox that wants to be a wolf! Legend: black star – A fox organization; grey star – A wolf organization

A firm that has ambitions of producing wolf product needs to have an organization that is consistent with a wolf. As Fig. 11.7 shows, a wolf product with a fox organization would not only be a drag on outcomes, but sustainability of innovation would be in great danger.

---

[3] See, for example, Christensen (1997), Tesmer (2002) or Davila et al. (2005), among others.

11.4.3 Mapping the Organizational Alignment

Each market archetype has its own organizational needs, that are right for the market in which a product is in. Fig. 11.8 summarizes some of the main organizational characteristics that can be considered right for each of the archetypes.

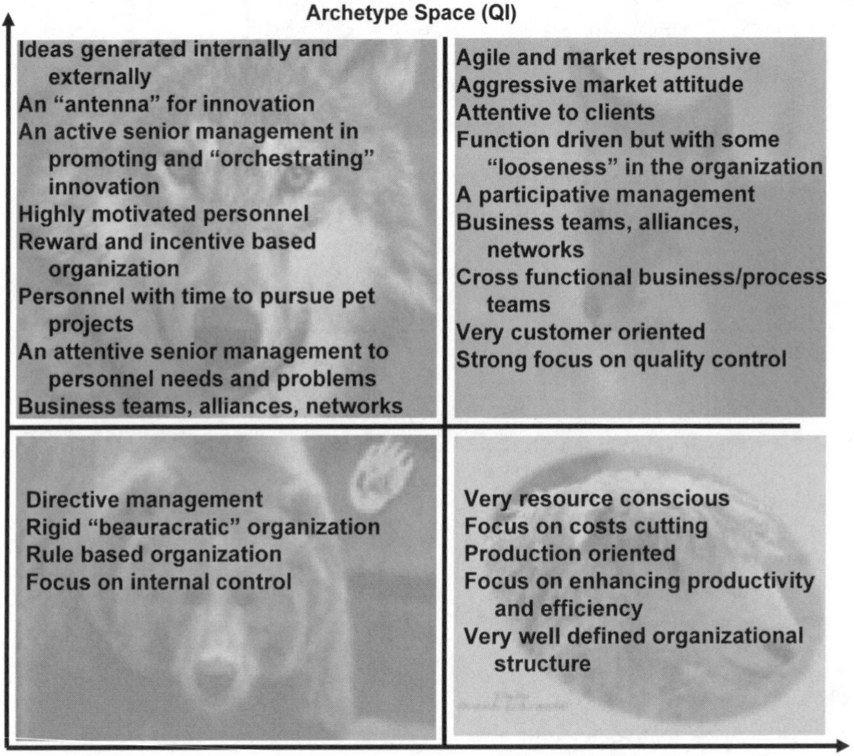

Fig. 11.8. Organization and Archetypes

A set of twenty questions comprises the assessment tool for identifying organizations in their archetypes. This survey can be done simultaneously or after the three other types of diagnostics (locus of product, cluster mapping and intrafirm-gap mapping) that we described in the previous chapter. For mapping organizational alignment, the results from the product diagnostics are required.

As in the product survey, the questions are scaled from 0 to 10. Some of the questions that we have designed for organizational diagnostics are given in Fig. 11.9 below.

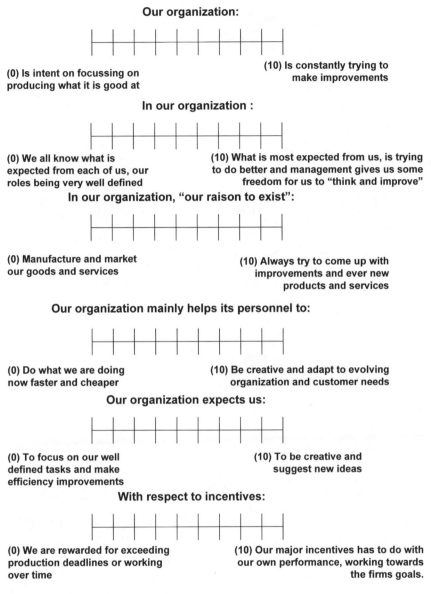

Our organization:

(0) Is intent on focussing on
producing what it is good at

(10) Is constantly trying to
make improvements

In our organization :

(0) We all know what is
expected from each of us, our
roles being very well defined

(10) What is most expected from us, is trying
to do better and management gives us some
freedom for us to "think and improve"

In our organization, "our raison to exist":

(0) Manufacture and market
our goods and services

(10) Always try to come up with
improvements and ever new
products and services

Our organization mainly helps its personnel to:

(0) Do what we are doing
now faster and cheaper

(10) Be creative and adapt to evolving
organization and customer needs

Our organization expects us:

(0) To focus on our well
defined tasks and make
efficiency improvements

(10) To be creative and
suggest new ideas

With respect to incentives:

(0) We are rewarded for exceeding
production deadlines or working
over time

(10) Our major incentives has to do with
our own performance, working towards
the firms goals.

Fig. 11.9. Organizational mapping

References

Abernathy WJ, Clark KB (1985) Innovation: Mapping the winds of creative destruction. Research Policy. 14: 3-22.

Abernathy WJ, Utterback JM (1978) Patterns of Innovation in Industry. Technology Review. 30(7): 40-47.

Acs ZJ, Audretsch DB (2003) Innovation and Technological Change. In Acs ZJ, Audretsch DB (Eds.). Handbook of Entrepreneurship Research, Kluwer Academic Publishers pp. 54-79.

Afuah N, Bahram N (1995) The hypercube of innovation. Research Policy 24: 51-76.

Ansoff I (1957) Strategies for Diversification. Harvard Business Review 35(5):113-124.

Archibugi D, Sirilli G (2001) The Direct Measurement of Technological Innovation in Business. In: European Commission Ed. Innovation and Enterprise Creation: Statistics and Indicators.

Battelle J (2005) The Search: How Google and Its Rivals Rewrote the Rules of Business and Transformed Our Culture. Portfolio Hardcover.

Birkinshaw J, Mol M (2006) How Management Innovation Happens. Management of Technology and Innovation. 47(4). pp. 81-88.

Bobrow EE, Shafer DW (1987) Pioneering New Products. McGraw-Hill Education.

Booz-Allen & Hamilton Inc (1982) New Product Management for the 1980s. New York. Booz Allen & Hamilton.

Brown LD, Plewes TJ, Gerstein MA (2004) Measuring Research and Development Expenditures in the U.S. Economy. Panel on Research and Development Statistics at the National Science Foundation, National Research Council.

Carr NG (2003) IT Doesn't Matter. Harvard Business Review.

Chandy R, Tellis GJ (1998) Organizing for Radical Product Innovation. Journal of Marketing Research. 35: 474-487.

Chesbrough HW (2005) Open Innovation: The New Imperative for Creating And Profiting from Technology. Harvard Business School Press.

Christensen CM (1997) The Innovator's Dilemma. Harvard Business School Press. Boston.

Christensen CM, Raynor ME (2003) The Innovator's Solution: Creating and Sustaining Successful Growth. Harvard Business School Press. Boston.

Collins CC, Porras JI (1994) Built to Last: Successful Habits of Visionary Companies. HarperCollins.

Cooper RG (2001) Winning at New Products - Accelerating the Process from Idea to Launch. 3rd Edn. Product Development Institute.

Cumming BS (1998) Innovation Overview and Future Challenges. European Journal of Innovation Management 1(1): 21-29.

Davila T, Epstein MJ, Shelton R (2005) Making Innovation Work: How to Manage It, Measure It, and Profit from It. Wharton School Publishing.

Drucker P (1993) Innovation and Entrepreneurship. 1st Edn. Collins.

Fast Company (2001) Why Can't Lego Click? 50:144.

Foster R (1986) Innovation: The attacker's advantage. London. MacMillan.

Franklin C (2003) Why Innovation Fails: Hard-Won Lessons for Business. Spiro Press.

Freeman C, Soete L. (1997) The Economics of Industrial Innovation. Pinter, London. 3rd Edn.

Friedman TL (2005) The World Is Flat: A Brief History of the Twenty-first Century. Farrar, Straus and Giroux.

Gartner WB (1989) "Who is an entrepreneur?" Is the wrong question. Entrepreneurship Theory & Practice 13(4): 47-68.

Gatignon H, Tushman ML, Sith W, Anderson P (2002) A Structural Approach to Assessing Innovation: Construct Development of Innovation Locus, Type, and Characteristics. Management Science 48(9): 1103-1122.

Gordon RJ (2000) Does the New Economy Measure Up to the Great Inventions of the Past? Journal of Economic Perspectives, 4(14): 49-74.

Grupp H (1998) Foundations of Economic of Innovation – Theory, Measurement and Practice. Edward Elgar, London.

Hansen JA (2001) Technology Innovation Indicator Surveys. In: Jankowski JE, Link AN, Vonortas NS Eds. Strategic Research Partnership.

Hauknes J (1999) Services in Innovation – Innovation in Services. Realising the Potential of the Service Economy: Facilitating Growth, Innovation and Competition, OECD Business and Industry Policy Forum, available at http://www.oecd.org/dataoecd/26/52/1827114.pdf.

Have ST, ten Wouter H, Frnas S, van der EM (2003) Key Management Models. Prentice Hall – Pearson Education Limited.

Henderson RM, Clark KB (1990) Architectural innovation: The reconfiguration of existing product technologies and the failure of established firms. Administrative Science Quarterly. 35:9-30.

Hotelling H (1929) Stability in competition. Economic Journal 39: 41-57.

Jaruzelski B, Dehoff K, Bordia R (2006) Smart Spenders: The Global Innovation 1000. Strategy & Business. Issue 45.

Kandybin A, Kihn M (2004) Raising Your Return on Innovation Investment. Available at http://www.strategy-business.com/resilience/rr00007?pg=all.

Kaplan RS, Norton DP (2004) Strategy Maps: Converting Intangible Assets into Tangible Outcomes. Harvard Business School Press.

Kirkpatrick D (2006) The world's most modern management – in India. Fortune. 14th April.

Leifer R, McDermott CM, O'Connor GCi, Peters LS, Rice MP, Veryzer RW (2000) Radical Innovation: How Mature Companies Can Outsmart Upstarts. Harvard Business School Press. Boston.

Licht G, Ebling G, Janz N, Niggemann H (1999) Innovation in service sector – Selected facts and some policy conclusions. Center for European Research. Manheim.

Metcalfe B (1999) Invention Is a Flower, Innovation Is s Weed. MIT Technology Review. pp. 54-57.

Minniti M, Bygrave WD, Autio E (2006) Global Entrepreneurship Monitor, 2005 Executive Report, Babson College and London Business School.

Moore G (1999) Crossing the Chasm. HarperBusiness.

Muller A, Välikangas L, Merlyn P (2005) Metrics for Innovation: Guidelines for Developing a Customized Suite of Innovation Metrics. Strategy & Leadership. 33. Woodside Institute.

Muller A, Välikangas L, Merlyn P (2005) Metrics for innovation: guidelines for developing a customized suite of innovation metrics. Strategy & Leadership 33(1) pp. 37 – 45.

National Science Fountadion (2005) The Task force on the future of American innovation, available at http://www.futureofinnovation.org/PDF/ Benchmarks _ PR.pdf.

OECD (2005) Proposed Guidelines for Collecting and Interpreting Technological Innovation available. Oslo Manual, available at http://www.oecd.org/ document/ 1/0,2340,en_2649_201185_33847553_1_1_1_1,00.html.

Peters TJ, Waterman RH (1982) In Search of Excellence: Lessons from America's Best-run Companies. HarperBusiness.

Porter ME (1998) Competitive Advantage: Creating and Sustaining Superior Performance. Free Press.

Rogers EM (1962) Diffusion of Innovations. Free Press.

Sarkar S (2005) Innovation and market structures: an integrated approach. International Journal of Innovation and Entrepreneurship Management, Vol 5, pp. 366-378.

Schacht WN (2000) The National Council for Science and the Environment, Industrial Competitiveness and Technological Advancement: Debate Over Government Policy, Brief for US Congress.

Schumpeter JA (1934) The Theory of Economic Development. Harvard University Press.

Schumpeter JA (1939) Business Cycles. McGraw-Hill Books Co. New York. pp. 87-88.

Schumpeter JA (1942) The Process of Creative Destruction.

Shenkar O (2004) The Chinese Century: The Rising Chinese Economy and Its Impact on the Global Economy, the Balance of Power, and Your Job. Wharton School Publishing.

Sundbo J, Gallouj F (1999) Innovation in Services in seven European Countries. Synthesis Report for European Commission, DG XII, TSER-SI4S.

Tarde G (1903) The Laws of Imitation. New York, Henry, Holt and Co.

Tesmer JA (2002) Your Perfect Business Match: A Groundbreaking Approach to Surviving and Thriving in Today's Business Battleground. Career Press.

Tidd J, Bessant J, Pavitt K (2005) Managing Innovation: Integrating Technological, Market Organizational Change. 3rd edn. John Wiley & Sons.

Tirole J (1988) The Theory of Industrial Organization. The MIT Press.

Tushman ML, Anderson PC, O'Reilly C (1997) Technology cycles, innovation streams, and ambidextrous organizations: organizational renewal through innovation streams and strategic change. In: Tushman ML and Anderson PC (eds) Managing strategic innovation and change: a collection of readings. NY. Oxford University Press.

Van Ark B, Broesma L, Hertog, dP (2003) Services Innovation, Performance Policy: A Review. Synthesis Report in the Framework of the Project Structural Information Provision on Information in Services.

Vise D, Malseed M (2005) The Google Story. Delacorte Press.

von Hippel E (2005) Democratizing Innovation. The MIT Press.

von Hippel, E (2005) Democratizing Innovation. MIT Press.

Warner F (2005) The Power of the Purse: How Smart Companies are Adapting to the World's Most Important Consumers. Prentice Hall.

Index